THE PLAYWRIGHT'S SURVIVAL GUIDE

KEEPING THE DRAMA IN YOUR WORK AND OUT OF YOUR LIFE

GARY GARRISON

HEINEMANN
PORTSMOUTH, NH

Heinemann
A division of Reed Elsevier Inc.
361 Hanover Street
Portsmouth, NH 03801–3912
www.heinemanndrama.com

Offices and agents throughout the world

The author and publisher wish to thank those who have generously given permission to reprint borrowed material:

"I've Been to the Dark Side" first appeared in the *Dramatists Guild Newsletter*, April/May 1998.

"Submitting Your Plays" first appeared in the *Dramatists Guild Newsletter*, Summer 1997.

"T-Minus-10 and Counting" first appeared in the *Dramatists Guild Newsletter*, January/February 1999.

"Just . . . Think on It" first appeared in the *Dramatists Guild Newsletter*, August 1998.

"Just . . . Passing It On" first appeared in the *Dramatists Guild Newsletter*, January/February 1998.

"Behave!" first appeared in the *Dramatists Guild Newsletter*, October 1997.

Kind thanks to Eve Corey for permission to use her painting, *Big Blue*, on the cover of this book. Ms. Corey has exhibited her work throughout the United States and lives and works in coastal Maine.

The Dramatists Guild of America is the only professional association for playwrights, composers, and lyricists. Guided by an elected Council, which gives its time, interest, and support for the benefit of writers everywhere, the Guild works to advance the rights of its more than six thousand members spanning the globe. Membership is open to all dramatic writers, regardless of their production history. For an application form, please contact the Membership Department at 1501 Broadway, Suite 701, New York, NY 10036.

Library of Congress Cataloging-in-Publication Data
Garrison, Gary.
    The playwright's survival guide : keeping the drama in your work and out of your life / Gary Garrison.
    p. cm.
    ISBN 0-325-00165-0
    1. Playwriting. 2. Playwriting—Vocational guidance. I. Title.
PN1661.G37   1999
808.2—dc21
                                 99-27323
                                 CIP

Editor: Lisa A. Barnett
Production: Vicki Kasabian
Cover design: Jenny Jensen Greenleaf
Cover painting: Eve Corey, *Big Blue*
Author photo: John Williams III
Manufacturing: Louise Richardson

Printed in the United States of America on acid-free paper
03 02 01 00   DA   2 3 4 5

For Michel, for all things great and small

Contents

PART 3

Acknowledgments

Special thanks go to Janet Neipris, for her words of support, kindness, and encouragement and for making the introduction to Richard Garmise, Jeff Zadroga and Greg Bosler at the Dramatists Guild. Without that introduction and those folks encouraging me, I would never have started writing about writing. I'm indebted to Jason Garret, my assistant and co-editor at NYU for his careful reading, thoughtful support, and caring words of advice. I marvel at your brilliance, Jason. Lisa Barnett, the editor of this book, deserves hearty thanks for her interest, excitement, and enthusiasm.

Thanks to the students at NYU's Dramatic Writing Program, who taught me as much about playwriting as I ever taught them, and to the teachers I challenged throughout my own education to teach me more, more, more, especially Milan Stitt and Zelma Weisfeld. I could never have been as honest as I am in this book without the help and advice of all the folks on Greenwich Street. And I am always grateful to my friend Pauline Gagnon for teaching me years ago how to organize my thoughts and write with some intelligence. Douglas Sills, Michael Walling, June Neal, and my agent, Fifi Oscard: I will never forget your support, encouragement, and enlightenment.

Big thanks to the folks in ATHE (Association for Theatre in Higher Education), Cathy Norgren and KC-ACTF (Kennedy Center's American College Theatre Festival), and the faculty and staff of NYU's Dramatic Writing Program for their undying support of new plays and playwrights. Finally, to those who inspire me, move my heart, and shake laughter from me daily: Michel, Zoe, Wendy, Rocco, Leslie, Marcy, Maggie, Stosh, Mom, and Dad.

Introduction

For Words

Here I sit, typical me—socks on with holes the size of golf balls (more hole than sock), wearing running shorts without a shred of elastic to hold them up, sporting a once-white T-shirt that was washed with a black shag bath mat, wearing my "I'd-never-be-caught-dead-in-these" eyeglasses and—in front of my computer on a church-quiet Sunday morning. I'm greeted by my old nemesis: the blank page. The white of the screen is so bright, I wince. I take a quick body check: yep, it's all there—headache, backache, and this wave of nausea that rises and falls. It all makes sense; I'm sitting down to write the first pages of this book.

If I made a list of all those things I needed or wanted to do in the next five years, writing a book would be, oh, maybe Number Thirty-Seven. So let me hit the obvious question right up front: Why? Why take the time? Why this instead of writing a new play or rewriting an old one? Because some hopeful kid out in Nebraska, who took his first playwriting course at a community college and wrote his first play and is busting-at-the-seams proud of, is sitting around on his own church-quiet Sunday morning saying, "Now what?"

Or because a woman in Tennessee works in a mall as a manager for the Gap by day, then races home to finish the fifth draft of her romantic comedy by night. It takes her an hour to forget her insecurities but two seconds to remember her dream. Each time she sits down at her keyboard she has to find enormous courage and raw strength to face her play and believe, honestly believe in her gut, there's a life for her play beyond the kitchen table.

Or because writing for the theatre is not nearly as difficult as getting produced is, and there are no quick answers to share, only experiences. Or because there are too many books on "How To" and none on "How to Be." Or because we're losing generations of playwrights and artists from our theatres because they can't see the value of writing for the theatre in the shadow of Hollywood. Or because I'd be selfish if I didn't: I've done too much, learned too much, hurt too much, and succeeded enough not to share what I know to be some fundamental truths about being an artist and a playwright. Or, finally, because I've been taught by the best how to write a play—but everyone forgot to tell me how to be a playwright.

In October 1997, Jeff Zadroga asked me to write an article for the *Dramatists Guild Newsletter*—something, he explained, to help the general membership of the Dramatists Guild, a service organization for writers in the theatre, understand the life of the aspiring writer and the business of playwriting from a real I-haven't-made-it-yet-but-just-give me-a-few-more-years point of view. I wrote what was fresh on my mind: "Submitting Your Plays: The Most Necessary Evil."

The idea for the article came in tandem with a modestly successful production (meaning, more than fifty people came) in New York of my play *When a Diva Dreams* and the feeling that the time was finally right to let the rest of the world in on it. Instantly I had three huge awakenings after my first round of submissions and rejections: (1) It's no longer good enough just to be an artist with art to peddle—you have to be a business person and a damn good one; (2) you can be both a playwright with a good play and a damn good business person and still get nowhere; and (3) you get nowhere even faster if you depend on your brother's best friend's sister's next-door neighbor who once worked at Seattle Rep to take your play to her boyfriend's accountant's wife who is the literary manager for the We Don't Have a Name Yet Theatre Company.

So, I methodically, almost scientifically, set out to submit the play to every appropriate theatre I could find through research. Being anal-retentive, I made charts and graphs, logged responses from literary managers, wrote thank-you letters, and plunged my hands in cold water whenever I wanted to write fuck-you letters.

The results of my yearlong "study" were enlightening, disheartening, oddly encouraging, and always frightening. I shared all of this in the *DGN* article, and I wrote it from a place that is hard for all of us—especially me—to touch: a position of honesty.

No one was more surprised than I at the response to this article. Cards, letters, phone calls, and chance conversations with fellow playwrights convinced me that I had written the article "right," or honestly (this from the guy whose mantra had always been "why speak the truth when a small lie makes us all feel better?"). Greg Bossler, the editor of the *Newsletter*, reacted favorably to the article and asked me to write what amounted to a series of articles on anything I wanted as long as I kept my honesty and sense of humor in play. So I wrote what was in my heart, struggled with every demon I've ever had, and set out to share some good, old-fashioned advice mixed with the practical nuts and bolts of how to be a surviving writer once you've written your play. 'Cause it's all about knowing how to stay healthy in your art once you've taken your fingers off the keyboard.

The first title of this book was *How to Keep Sane and Productive and Happy and Content and Still Writing and Growing and Nurturing Yourself as an Artist and Not Want to Kill Your Mother, Father, Brother, Sister, Wife, Husband, Companion, or Dog While You're Waiting for the "Theatre by the Bay and Bakery" to Finally Say "YES! We're Producing Your Play,"* because there are two sides to the experience of being a playwright: the heart side and the head side. Your heart has to learn how to sustain your soul while your head figures out the craft and skills of playwriting at the exact same time you're trying to push your career up a steep, slippery mountain. That's a tall order by anybody's definition. So this is not a book on how to write a play; this is a book on how to be a surviving playwright. And it's my simple theory that you have to keep the drama in your work and out of your life to be a successful playwright. Let's get to it.

PART 1

To walk, we have to lean forward, lose our balance, and begin to fall.
We let go constantly of the previous stability, falling all the time, trusting
that we will find a succession of new stabilities with each step . . .
Our experience of the past, and of those dear to us, is not lost at all,
but remains richly within us . . .

Robin Skinner

✳   ✳   ✳

FOR YOUR HEART

(This is the stuff you want to think about when you're
doubting yourself or your talent, or wondering if you have
what it takes to be a playwright.)

✳   ✳   ✳

You're the Play

Ask anybody who knows me: I'm peculiar. But I guess no more peculiar than the guy standing right beside me at the deli this morning who ordered his coffee black, then dumped seven packets of sugar in the cup, lidded it, shook it up, dumped two more packets of sugar in, shook it up, then added real cream and a teaspoon of powdered cream to the mix, shook it up, and finished it off with a half cup of hot water. I thought, he's not buying a cup of coffee, he's building it. He paid for his coffee and asked for two more packets of sugar. My mouth dried out. I got queasy. If I drank that cup of coffee, you'd have to peel me off the ceiling of my office with a putty knife.

I walked out of the deli, saw the Sugar Man hail a cab with a nod of his head, and watched him as he pulled open the door with a strained extension of his left little finger. He backed into the cab, butt first, and just as he was about to close the cab door, kicked his feet together to shake the dirt from his shoes. The door closed and the cab sped off. What a peculiar man, I thought. What a peculiar, fascinating, intriguing man with his sugar and shaking shoes. Then I thought: who's watching me, thinking the same thing?

Convinced that great drama was composed of characters that were quirky, odd, and unusual, I spent years as a young writer absorbed in the peculiarities of *other* people. It never occurred to me if I took an honest look at all that was quirky, odd, and peculiar about *myself*, I'd have the resource to write any character or story I'd ever want to create. The challenge is, of course, daring yourself to look deep inside and discover what it is about you that can become the genesis for all your drama instead of making it up from an overburdened imagination. When I finally learned how to do just that, my writing deepened and defined itself in a way I never thought possible. Follow my personal story to see how it came out on the other side of my writing.

I grew up in big bayou country, baby. Yeah, huuuunneeeeee. Southeast Texas. Just a button of a town with Tons O' Baptists. Big Bar-b-quin' folk who store herds of cattle in freezers and wait for a social lull. A place where a Dairy Queen and a Burger King stand as royal rural monuments to hormone-raging, acne-bearing teenagers who need a place to work and flirt. A day out on the town meant strolling Sears & Roebuck looking for a tighter fit in underwear. Think *The Last Picture Show* meets George Wallace (before the apology), marries Tammy Faye Baker, mates with the cast of Hee-Haw, and gives birth to any character in any Tennessee Williams play—you get the idea.

I was raised in a good family and community of God-fearing, hardworking, middle-class southerners where (1) football and religion were one and the same; (2) if you could fry it, it was on your dinner table; (3) cowboy boots were an extension of the foot; (4) triple-decker shotgun racks were a necessity for your Made-Only-In-America truck; (5) the drawl was so thick you couldn't cut it with a thesaurus; and (6) desirable home collectibles included little clay figures of pre–Civil War African Americans with exaggerated, bright red lips and molded in various stages of repose.

Into this world I was born—clearly an alien. And from my baby steps onward, I was destined not to be your typical southern boy. In my neck of the woods, *that* meant certain, guaranteed heartache. If you played with sock puppets instead of plastic army men, or staged theatrical extravaganzas behind your father's toolshed instead of playing stage coach in your kiddy wagon, you were destined for a Big Butt-Kickin'. If you shied away from all things "boy," like hunting, fist-fighting, watching football on TV, trading baseball cards, playing King of the Mountain, or killing frogs with a BB gun, you set your own stage for Tough Times with guys named Big Earl or Bubba.

And "set the stage" I did. Early on, I figured if I was going to be different, I was going to go the distance. I was going to be the poster child for the southern and Socially Impaired. Ninety-nine percent of my high school friends were on the Triple A-string of this or that contact sport—anything that required a jock strap. I was a cheerleader. Yep, the only male cheerleader in literally a five-hundred mile radius of my hometown, and the only white cheerleader my freshmen year. You

4

could say I made quite a few names for myself—some I'm proud of, some still hurt. And of course, my brothers were All-Star football players for our high school and All-State somethings. I cheered them all the way to the top from a place very far down in my rebellious soul.

As a final insult to injury: I was a natural actor/performer/comedian. I had to be: I was—as we say in the South—"butt ugly," with kinky, curly blond hair, bad teeth, raging acne, and a gangly, awkward body. I *had* to make 'em laugh to forgive or forget the side of me I couldn't hide. Naturally, I was the kid in the back of the class making the squealing pig noises behind his book, or telling dirty jokes to the Student Body president during a Crime Prevention seminar that made him laugh so hard he uncontrollably farted four times in a row, or burping during the final "Amen" of the school prayer. I tried out for every school play, acting like I was an actor. Sometimes I was cast, other times not. But each time I gave an audition that no one would forget.

I was different. I was fearless. The combination was sure to injure me—but it never stopped me. Nothing could. Not even my family. *"Lord, the things I put my people through . . . my poor family. I've been the spoon that stirs their pot like nobody's business . . ."* That's a line from one of my plays, and as with all of my writing, straight from my life. During all that craziness from elementary through high school, my family stood by me—or, at least, I think I felt them there. They must have loved me, because they didn't kill me. And I gave them plenty of reason to. They quietly understood my "difference" and negotiated it within their own souls. And though I'm sure I was as much a puzzle to them as they were to me at times, they rarely refused to allow *me* to be *me*. If you're lucky, that's what you get from your first family.

I left home in the mid-70s to study acting. I was eighteen and floating from one makeshift, well-intentioned undergrad theatre/dance/music/communications department to another. In each, I found or created my family again: my father was in every strong-willed, determined director I worked with; my brothers appeared as those ever-rugged techies I secretly admired and stood in awe of; my mother was every costumer I worked with—sizing me up and knowing every dark secret I managed to keep from the world, noting my flaws then gently hiding them in some form of fashion; and me. I was there in every actor I saw, throwing out every emotion I had on stage, begging for someone or anyone's approval. Eventually, I would move on, only to create "family" in the next academic or professional theatre I wound up in. I guess that's what we do in the theatre: we create family, then leave them for good, on a regular basis.

When I finished muddling my way through countless professional theatres as an actor and happened into a Ph.D. program at the University of Michigan, someone new crept into my family: *writers*. I wasn't so quick to let them in. I mean, they looked weird, they acted weird, they talked about things I never heard of, and they wrote weird shit. Yet there was something about them I was drawn to: these scribes, these word-jerkers knew my torment, all my fears, my countless anxieties, and my handful of dreams. It was in their work, their words. I came to understand that that was a writer's job—to know me; to put my life up to my face, say, "take a look, cheerleader," and make me feel something. Wow. Acting never came close to that. Directing seemed even more removed. But writing plays . . .

God, I wanted to become one of them. Desperately. So I did. Slowly. Painfully. Quietly, so no one would notice. I'd been working in the theatre almost twelve years only to discover that what I was meant to be— who I really was—was a writer. Of course, I would never have gotten there without the experiences of acting, cheerleading, burping, and building families and tearing them down.

The work never came easy to me. For hours before writing a single word, I'd torture myself with doubts, insecurities, and this inexplicable need to have everything I wrote be perfect the first time. What kept me from totally paralyzing myself then, and even now, was a talk I had with a close friend as we sat in his car in the dead of winter with the heater up high (he couldn't pay his home heating bill), drinking Campbell's Chicken Noodle soup from a can and eating Cheese Cheetos with pink rubber gloves on so no powder residue could stick to our fingers. I explained to him that I couldn't think of anything to write for my playwriting class. I had spent days trying to think of something, nay, *anything* interesting, provocative, new, or daring. Nothing came. The more clever I tried to be the worse my writing got. Things were getting critical. I was regressing to a symbolism play using Jack, Jane, and Spot.

Finally, he tossed his Campbell soup can out the car window and into the garbage can, turned to me, and quietly said, "Why are you trying to make something up? With your history?! *You're* the play." I knew exactly what he meant, even though my "history" was only twenty-two years old.

That night I began writing *Does Anybody Want a Miss Cow Bayou?*, a monologue play about a nineteen-year-old girl from the southeast Texas bayou country who, knowing she's not attractive, talks like a hillbilly, and is considered "different" by everyone around her, enters the Miss Texas Pageant and shows up at the contest demanding to be one of the ten finalists that will appear on television. Armed with a shotgun for persuasion and a guitar in case the judges want to hear her sing, she pleads her case: she needs to be seen. She needs to be heard. She needs her family, who have given her up for adoption, to see her on television and . . . maybe want her.

The play was produced a month after I wrote it. A year later it was published by Buffalo Press. Since then it has been produced all over the country in a variety of venues, and every time I see it and hear the actress recite the line, "I knowed I ain't like them other girls. Hell, I never thought I had to be 'till I seen the sour look on all of your faces . . ." I swallow hard and relearn my first lesson in playwriting and being a playwright:

You're the play.

The success of *Miss Cow Bayou* comes down to one thing, folks: I'm Miss Cow Bayou. I'm that young girl from head to toe, heart to soul. She's got all my hurts, desperation, jealousy, ignorance, and fearlessness right there for you to take a long, painful gander at. It's almost shameful, it's so autobiographical. But the audience doesn't know that. What they see is a young woman who has very real needs and raw feelings just bubbling at the surface, who desperately wants something from those around her, and who receives the worst possible thing: their indifference. Who couldn't relate to that? I couldn't extract myself from that play if I wanted to.

Everyone's life is fascinating, unusual, and worth noting dramatically because all of us have big events that profoundly affect us or tiny, quiet moments that change our lives forever. Everyone has some secret that has to stay hidden, an oddity that defies explanation, or a curious relationship with the world. And we've got weird people in our lives: an uncle who has never been able to remember our names no matter how many times someone repeats it for him, a next-door neighbor who practices witchcraft and is the president of the local PTA, or a best friend who has an obsession with Brazil. We've all wondered why our local librarian dabs at her mouth with a Kleenex every time we walk in the door, then gives us a wink when we walk out; why the guy at the car wash reads his Bible while he's drying our car with a dirty rag, or why our minister stores the church money in ice cream cartons in his freezer. We are surrounded by fascinating people—ourselves included. And therein lies my second lesson in playwriting and being a playwright: *My own life can be the stuff of interesting drama.*

When I look back over all the plays I've written, I see that they're littered with everyone I've known, wanted to know or, sadly, would never know. No one is there more often than me, with my issues, big heartaches, and joyful celebrations shining like a beacon inside the smallest monologue or ten-minute play. My "stuff" oozes out of every word I write for every character I create. And I'm convinced that whatever success I've had in this career is directly related to my ability to say in my work, "Damn! It hurts when your best friend betrays you" in such a way that you'll respond, "I know what you mean."

Why spend a frigging eternity trying to innovate or fabricate the emotional life of a character in your play when what is so special and precious about you, the thing that makes you the object of all kinds of interesting reactions from different people, is enough to create a compelling character or a dramatically riveting story? Alright, so you haven't swum the seven seas, taken an apartment in Venice just for the inspiration of the view, been an intern on Capitol Hill, had a torrid affair with someone whose name you don't remember, or combed the back hills of Tennessee looking for the definitive log cabin. If you've lived on the face of this earth for fifteen, twenty, twenty-five years, or longer, and if you've listened to your own life stories as they've unfolded, you have all the dramatic material you'll ever need for a lifetime of writing.

We're complex beings that *no one* understands but *everyone's* trying to understand. That's why we write. We're trying to make sense of ourselves. And if what we write for the theatre are *people* in dramatic situations and not the reverse, doesn't it make sense that you'd want to understand more of yourself and use yourself as the catalyst for any art you create? Look, I need every shortcut I can find when I write. If I know I'm carrying around a tremendous resource for dramatic material inside of me, how dumb am I not to use it? Not that dumb.

Will I ever understand what family is? I don't know. But clearly I keep trying to answer that question over and over again in my playwriting. That little boy who grew up in bayou country and swatted away every social convention, replacing it with in-your-face daring and courage, who challenged and almost defied his family to love him then looked for family in every theatre experience he had, needs to know the answer. So here I sit, with all my plays, following the "what is family" thread woven inextricably through them all—and I am thankful that I have some mechanism for exorcizing my demons and celebrating my enlightenment. Thank God I'm a playwright.

Skippy, Jake, and the Spitfire Within

One day a couple of years ago, a really talented student named Beth confessed to me that she grew up in an ultra-repressed, very tight social structure and that her family was—by all accounts—of the Jekyll and Hyde variety, meaning in public they were Perfect Parents with three children: Happy, Happier, and Happiest. But in private, they were miserable people who tried to avoid one another like a reoccurrence of athlete's foot.

Beth survived her teen years, she explained, by allowing the fun-loving, hell-raising side of her personality to surface in the guise of a playful alter ego: Skippy. Skippy was a big, out-of-control mess. Skippy would act out in a grand way. She would shoot her mouth off at any authority figure (teachers, principals, police, ministers, representatives of the Red Cross), ignore all traffic signs on any public road (why go 30 mph when going 70 blurs an unattractive landscape?), escape her house at midnight and return by dawn with some article of clothing conspicuously missing—in short, do anything to shamelessly flirt with being arrested, suspended from school, or humiliated in public.

I confessed to Beth that although we grew up years and miles apart from each other, Skippy had a long-lost, older, third cousin that went with me everywhere: Jake. It wasn't me who gave Lori Hood a hickey the size of a dinner plate—it was Jake. Jake thought all the guys would think he was cool if he had that much passion/suction. No, I would never even think of dating three people who shared the same nine-by-twelve-foot office at the bank I worked for. Jake, though, thought he could get away with it—and you know what, he did—until he was busted by his supervisor, who put it all together. That Jake was a rascal. He was the one who told the college professor teaching a course in the New Testament that the reason he didn't study for the final exam was because he decided to convert to Judaism, and it seemed inappropriate to know so much about the New Testament. He was the one who forced me to stand on a tabletop in front of four hundred University of Michigan communications majors, drop my pants to reveal white satin boxer shorts with red hearts, and proceed with a lecture on semiotics. It wasn't me. Uh-uh. I don't have that kind of courage.

Talking about our playful alter egos, Beth and I discovered another similarity: Skippy and Jake got older, wiser, and meaner. They turned on us. They no longer pushed us into doing things we'd never consider doing ourselves, but instead became the voice for our doubts, insecurities, codependencies, and any other emotional junk we refused to face. And because they knew us so well, they knew where it would hurt the most. And they went right there. Right to the Hurt Spot. We couldn't escape them if we tried, and the harder we tried, the more vocal they became. When I was studying acting, Jake would pipe in with this monologue:

> What are you doing? You don't know how to act. You're a fraud. Everyone can see you can't act. You're embarrassing. Where's your pride, man? Don't you care what people think of you? Get out while you can. You're losing your hair, for God's sake. You're twenty, and you look forty. What are you going to do, play all the grandpa roles? Now, that's a career.

When I decided to study directing in graduate school, Jake kicked into overdrive:

> See? I told you acting wasn't for you. But what do you know about directing? You can't even get your dog, Bowser, to sit when you say "sit." How the hell are you going to get people to cross the stage when you want them to? And you don't know shit about dramatic literature. So what are you going to direct? You don't have the background, pal. You don't have the intelligence or sensitivity. You don't have the people skills. I mean, for God's sake, you've never even read *The Empty Room*.

But he was never as sharp, or hurtful and persistent, as when I decided to be a writer:

> Oh, great. Great! Hey, if this doesn't work out, try being a lighting designer, because that's all that's left. A writer? Are you joking? Oh, this is painful. You really want to fail, don't you? What the hell do you

know about writing? Everyone's been reading *The Poetics* while you've been doing "Dames At Sea." And do you really think you have something interesting to say? And you're from the South for God's sake. Tennessee Williams already wrote the South. Well, whatever you do, I'm begging you not to write about love, sex, relationships, God, politics, the environment, science, math, culture, or religion. Stick to what you know: food.

Jake's voice and those scripts are still as familiar to me as my thumbprint. So how did I kick his butt out of my life? First, I tried to disarm him by trying harder, working faster, and thinking quicker, but that didn't work for long. What finally drove him out was defining for *myself* what being a writer meant to me, and then living the definition. And it was *my* definition. No one else's. Not a teacher's, not another playwright's, or a friend's, or family's.

A lot of my students, or other drama jocks just beginning their journey in dramatic writing, often ask, "How do I know if I'm a writer?"— as if you could look at their feet, see a sixth toe, and say, "Oh, there's your proof." It's not that simple to answer. But it's also not a "you'll know" kind of thing, either. So here's my definition of who a writer is.

Somebody who has something important they want to say and is passionate about saying it. If you're jello writing it, I'm jello reading it. It starts by caring about something, *anything*, in the world that really grinds your wheels and then wanting desperately to share what you feel for your audience's enlightenment or understanding. Technique and craft are subjective: I can like or dislike how you end act 1, but I'll care less about how and what you do mechanically if I'm riveted by what you say and by the emotional intensity of how you're saying it.

Somebody who loves and cherishes the process as much as they do the product. Look, we all like to write good plays. But they don't just happen on us. A play has to be shaped, molded, deconstructed, reconceived, evaluated, thrown away, retrieved from the trash, cried over, thrown against the wall, thought over, laughed over, rehashed and finally admired. I know only one writer (and even he is questionable) that has the talent to crank out a first draft of a play and say, "it's done."

12

Writing is a process, and often a long process that requires making huge mistakes. When I've met a writer that's not interested in the process, I've met a writer that's not interested in a career.

Somebody who can receive criticism and keep his/her ego in check. Doesn't that sound obvious? You'd think it would be. But writers get into that "I know better than you because this is *my* baby, *my* soul, *my* story" bullshit and they can't see the forest for the trees. Alright, I admit nobody knows my play like I know my play, but I have to force my ego to be smaller than my desire to get the play right. I'm not an expert (as if there were one in the theatre). I want your feedback because I don't want to just leave it up to chance that you get my ideas or my story. And if you've got something to say about my play that will, at the very least, get me thinking, baby, bring it on.

Somebody who can rewrite. See above: passion, process, criticism. If you're dying to share something with me, and you embrace the process and listen to what I may have to offer about your play, then rewriting becomes the natural expression of just how much you care about it all.

Somebody who is disciplined and self-motivated. Writers write. That's what they do. You have to have that drive, that need that pulls you back to your keyboard time and time again, when oftentimes you have nothing to be writing for except your own enjoyment. God knows the rewards can be few and far between. But you write because you have to, because no other form of expression would salve your wound or celebrate your discovery.

We all come to the experience in different ways, with different life stories. Only you know what it takes to drag yourself away from watching the one-hundredth rerun of *Cheers* to get to the keyboard. Only you know how many bathtubs and sinks you'll wash and closets you'll straighten before you get down to writing. Only you know the phone calls you'll make instead of doing the work. You can't bake lasagna and call it a play.

Only you can write your play. If you want to write, nothing gets in your way. If you don't want to write—for whatever reason—a gun to your head won't make a difference. Find your way to write. The answer is in you, nobody else.

Somebody who knows the industry. We're going to talk about this further on, but for now, think about this: would you seriously consider being a gardener if you didn't know all the nurseries in your city, what kind of plants and flowers work best in humid weather, who's the best resource for dirt in your area, which businesses have their own in-house gardeners, and which businesses are always looking for someone new, someone with different ideas? If you answer "yes," then I can see you sitting on a deserted road with a big daffodil between your legs, looking north, looking south, and not knowing where the heck to plant it; the daffodil dies from lack of information and attention.

Somebody who reads. I have to say, I'm floored by the number of playwrights who don't read plays. Hello?! Can you imagine being a painter and not looking through books of art or visiting an art gallery? Can you imagine being a photographer and not knowing who created the trends in contemporary photography? Would a screenwriter never watch a film? a novelist never read great books? Don't we learn from one another? Isn't that the genesis for all education?

Playwrights can be snotty brats when it comes to reading the great works of dramatic literature. I don't get it. Are we just lazy, or do we think no one has anything to show us that we couldn't think up for ourselves? And I'm not talking about reading a play because you have to for a class. I'm talking about reading Ibsen, Beckett, Miller, O'Neill, Hellman, Wilson, Kushner, Wolfe, Wasserstein, Stoppard, or Hwang on your own time because they have something damn important to say that resonates in your soul as a writer. Every one of these writers, and the hundreds more not mentioned, can teach you everything you need to know about writing for the theatre.

Somebody who goes to the theatre. Yes, you have to see it live for the same reasons you have to read it.

Somebody who is a keen observer. Whatever form you're writing in, you're most likely writing about people. Human beings are complex—deeply contradictory, wildly controversial, intensely vulnerable. You're

14

never going to write a *situation* that is more interesting than the *people* involved in it.

When you get in an elevator, it's either going to go up, down, or stall. Sure, it may go up or down fast or slowly, or it may stall for hours, but that's pretty much all it's going to do. The story of an elevator moving or stalling is not particularly interesting until we know (1) that people are inside, and (2) exactly *who* those people are. I guarantee you that if my mother, your mother, her father, and the local Catholic bishop are in the elevator, the story will be different than if I'm trapped in there with you, Michael Jackson, Tammy Faye Baker, and Newt Gingrich—and each story will be worth telling.

So if you're going to write people, you've got to watch people to figure out what human behavior looks like in relation to its emotional foundation. You've got to probe the human psyche and figure out why that waitress at your local coffee shop bends pieces of paper into tiny squares, then shoots them with her middle finger at the framed face of Ronald Reagan.

Somebody who writes for the theatre. To me, live theatre has no emotional equivalent for any writer. It's gloriously dangerous, unnervingly unpredictable, and tremendously exhilarating when it works because it's happneing in real-life time. You write for the theatre:

- □ because there's a live audience that is as much a part of the experience of your play as any central character, and you get juiced when you think of the audience watching the play and laughing themselves silly or tearing up at the end of act 1.
- □ because you recognize that actors are not machines, and that each night something terrifying and new will happen on stage. But that's OK with you because you learn something new every night about your work.
- □ because you enjoy an art form that is reliant on good communication between artists, technicians, and administrators and recognize that to produce your small play takes a giant collaboration, and you like being a part of a team.
- □ because no other medium would serve your idea. Television would be too close and film even closer. A novel would be too

removed and a short story would only begin to tell the tale. The theatre gives your message the distance *and* closeness it needs to be heard.

☐ because the event being "live" means anything could happen and often does, and there's something about that risk and danger that excites you.

☐ because you like the fact that you can change the script until closing night, tweaking the play to within an inch of its life.

☐ because at the end of the night, your play evaporates and all that is left is the message you placed in the minds of your audience. They can't replay it on videotape, order it up on a cable channel, check it out at Blockbuster, turn back to page one to understand what's happening on page 210, or start the CD over. Your play lives in the mind of that audience . . . and that feels good to you.

That's my definition of a writer. And as long as I keep it close to my heart and always present in my creative soul, I can tell Jake to kiss my big, southern, bayou butt good-bye. Put your Skippy and Jake to rest. It's time. They take too much energy and they're destructive as hell. Give 'em the boot. There's no room in your creative soul for both of you. Tell them Gary and Beth sent you.

Thump It Before You Buy It

I can still see my sweet mama—tall, thin, ladylike, hair done, face done, patent leather purse dangling on a crooked arm—making her way through the produce section of the local Piggly Wiggly, touching, squeezing, smelling and patting every piece of fruit on the shelf. As a small kid it was very confusing to see my mother's intimate, tactile relationship with fruit. I couldn't figure out what she was doing, but it looked like fun, so inevitably she'd find me in the vegetable section slapping some zucchini senseless.

My favorite part was when she'd thump the watermelons. One day, after seeing the intense "what are you doing?" look on my face, she said, "Huuneey, thuuuump it before you buy it." Then she attacked a big, striped watermelon with her index finger, thumping it to within an inch of its shelf life. She went on to explain that if it sounded good (translation: if the thump resonated inside), it'd taste good. Who knew then that she was teaching the forty-two-year-old me how to listen to criticism of my plays.

The bottom line is, we want some people to like our play. What am I saying—we want *everybody* to *love* our play, no matter how unreasonable that sounds. But some people aren't going to like it, and some (usually our best friends) are not even going to get it. However, if you've asked someone to read your play, or invited a group of people to listen to a reading of your play, you're *obligated* to graciously listen to what they have to say about it in response. They, on the other hand, are obligated to be sensitive to your needs as a writer.

Don't you want to smack people who think they know how to write your play? Don't you want to die when someone who's talking about your play goes on and on and on and on and on and has only five more points they want to make before they finally shut up? Don't you really hate when someone totally misses the point of a scene and tries to reason the logic of the play in front of you? Don't you want to take back every word you've said when you hear yourself defending or explaining your play? Don't you wish you'd stop apologizing for the play, or disclaiming it before it's even read? So do I. So I learned how to control the criticism. Yep. Control it. Make it work for me; thump it before I buy it.

Controlling criticism and the relationship between you and your reader/audience is a simple idea that playwrights, for some reason, forget they have the power to do. After all, we are nothing if not preemptive. It hurts when we're criticized harshly, and it's disappointing when we're not criticized enough. Here are some ways to ensure you get what you need from the reader's or audience's response and to keep them well behaved when you've asked them to read or listen to your play:

1. Don't prejudice your reader or audience before they read or hear your play. Avoid statements such as, "I hate the ending" (they will too), "I hate the character of Zoe" (they will too), "I don't think it's very funny (they won't either), "I just want to throw this whole damn thing away," (they'll want to, too), "this is really bad, but . . ." (so why did you ask them to read it or see it?). If you can't control your mouth go lock yourself in a closet until the play's read or heard.

2. Don't hand off the play to the reader or begin a discussion with the audience by saying, "I want you to rip it to shreds," or "Don't be afraid to be really critical." What are you, nuts? There's no valor in self-flagellation. And you're asking for it! And the truth is, not many writers can walk away from a discussion in which their play was "ripped to shreds" and recover creatively. There's a fragile artist's ego in all of us. Protect it. Touch your inner child, touch your navel if you have to, but don't ask to be slammed in the head for the sake of your art.

3. Once you finally sit down to talk to the reader or listen to feedback after a public reading, discreetly control the discussion, instead of allowing it to float all over the place Have five or six salient points to discuss, leaving time for your reader or audience to then offer anything not addressed. That way, you both feel satisfied. But, *don't monopolize* the discussion either. You've asked the reader or audience to talk, and they

want to talk, so let them talk. When a writer won't let me talk, I know they're not really interested or can't hear what I have to say.

4. If you find yourself having to explain too many things in the play, stop. Bottom line: it was either unclear to the reader/audience or unclear in the writing. Just make a note that something's not clear and move on. A discussion that involves a heavy dose of explanation on your part is not a discussion at all.

5. Don't be afraid to limit the amount of discussion. You can only absorb so much before it starts feeling very overwhelming. If the discussion becomes longer than the play, then you have more problems than you can clearly focus on at that moment. You can only hear so much; acknowledge your limitations.

6. Your only obligation when someone is discussing your play is to *listen* attentively to their comments. You don't have to like or agree with what they're saying, but you have to try to remain receptive and not become defensive. When you begin defending your choices, everyone becomes uncomfortable. All I ever ask from a playwright whose work I've read is to *consider* what I'm suggesting. If I sense you're not listening—for whatever reason—I'll stop talking. Later, in the quiet of your home, you can "thump it to see if you buy it."

7. If you've asked someone just to read your play, kindly suggest a time line for your reader. Make up some impending deadline if you have to (*"Manhattan Theatre Club wants to see the next draft . . ."*), but sink a date for the discussion and *leave them alone until then*. That's right: not a call, not a note, no "looks." If you mutually agree on a date to talk, you won't be wondering why they haven't called or why they look like they're avoiding you at work/home/rehearsal/the bar. You then have to honor the time line. If they don't honor the time line, give them a polite nudge. Usually that's all you need to do to set their guilt in motion. If they still don't respond, move on, and never ask that person to read your work again.

8. And for Your Future. Thank whoever read or listened to your play. Overdo it. Be big-time effusive. Pull the stops out. They did you a favor.

Be verbally grateful. And if you want them to read or hear the next draft, be *really* nice.

The first full-length play I ever wrote, (and which no one will ever see), is buried in a box out of the sight of humankind. I can't burn it—I'm too superstitious. I can't read it—it's too painful. I wouldn't dream of showing it to my best, best, best friend—she'd take too much pleasure in knowing how awful it is. It'll never see the light of day. Because it's not really my play, but a play written by committee. I listened to too many people who had too many big ideas about my small play. I took every single piece of criticism and advice that came toward me and applied it to my play, and eventually I lost sight of what I'd written. I'll never do that again; not as long as there's a watermelon around.

Sing Out, Louise!

I take nothing for granted. The title above is a line from the musical *Gypsy*, wherein an overbearing stage mother, Mama Rose, stands just off-stage barking orders to her introverted daughter who's auditioning for a producer. Mama Rose wants Louise to succeed in ways she can only dream of for herself. "Sing out, Louise" is part family anthem, but mostly smart, motherly advice for Louise if she ever wants to get a job. Louise, like so many artists, has all the talent in the world waiting to explode—but not a single skill to promote it.

I would feel more comfortable promoting the entire population of a third-world country than promoting myself. Ohhhhhh, God, it's sooooooo awkward. When I meet someone that I know could potentially help my career, I immediately feel like every orifice in my body is dripping something and it'll be just moments before the person faints dead away from the sight of the dripping, drooling horror that is me. So I've had to learn the hard way that your work can take you a good part of the way down the road, but you, the person, must deliver it to the Promised Land.

I'm not BS-ing you here. You've truly got to buck up, stand straight, talk right, and not behave like a heathen just escaped from More Tales of the Darkside. This is going to be a little harsh, but hopefully all you would-be playwrights will understand where it's coming from, so *listen up*!

I see you out there talking to people who can make or break your careers, and you act like an idiot! You say you want to be a writer, and you have a play to sell, but how far do you think you're going to get if you don't know squat about *selling yourself*? That's right, selling—your *self*, not just your art. And selling yourself means knowing yourself—the good, the bad, the ugly, the so ugly you can't believe it's you. *This is not negotiable*: you have to figure out who and what you are, learn to put your best self forward, and make people like you for the ten or fifteen minutes they're with you. If they like you, there's a good chance they'll want to read your plays. But I guarantee if they don't like you, you'll have to be a big name in theater before everyone forgets that you're a jerk and reads your plays anyway. So when you meet people in the industry, remember: you've got two objectives—get them interested in you and get them interested in your art.

Easier said than done, right? Absolutely. I can't argue that. And I don't have an answer for you, only my experiences. And those experiences tell me that nobody gets ahead in this business by hiding in a corner or behind a friend, waiting to be discovered. No one wants to interact with someone who can't form intelligible sentences yet professes to work in an art that's based in language. No one wants to talk to your ego. No one wants to have dinner with your bitterness. No one wants to spend twenty minutes with your verbal resume. No one's really impressed with who you know in the business. But everyone wants to have a good time. So in a social situation with people who can influence your career, walk the walk, talk the talk, and shoot the bullshit so high you'd wish you were wearing hip boots instead of Doc Martens.

If you're like me, presenting yourself positively to someone you don't know in the industry feels as unnatural and dirty as bathing in used bathwater. But you have to, so here are simple rules to follow:

Rule Number 1: **Look like a person that people want to talk to.** Whether you're at a quiet dinner party and one person just happens to be a literary manager of a theatre, at the opening of a new play at your local black box and someone introduces you to the artistic director, or on the street with a friend who introduces you to another friend that's in the business, you have to be a person people want to talk with, not avoid like tooth decay. How? Try to lower your guard (the one you put up routinely around industry people because you've been rejected so many times), look them in the eye (no one likes to talk to someone's hairline), and ease into a conversation that allows you to get a handle on the kind of person you're talking to.

I know, I know. It's hard for some folks. Some of us are real shy, some of us get nervous around people we don't know and just spit and sputter, and some of us just aren't gifted conversationalists. Add to that the element of pressure that this person could maybe do something for your career and you could easily fall to pieces after the first "hello." So here's some not-so-profound advice that's always worked for me: get them to talk about themselves by asking questions. This works for several reasons: (1) everyone loves to talk about themselves; (2) the focus is off you, giving you time to feel more comfortable; and (3) they will eventually feel obligated to ask you about yourself, and then you're home free. If you don't know how to start the conversation, be basic: "how'd you get to be a literary manager?"

Warning: Be genuine. Don't ask questions for the sake of asking questions. Don't ask questions, then not listen. Don't ask stupid questions. *Engage* in the conversation so it's not a monologue. And when the time's appropriate, and they've turned the focus on you, seize the opportunity . . . gently, and proceed to:

Rule Number 2: **Put your best foot forward**. That means, don't apologize for who you are, don't excuse your career and try to explain why you haven't made it to Broadway yet, don't lambast the industry they work in and rear your bitter head (they don't have enough misery in their lives they should have to listen to yours?) and for God's sake, don't make them have to pull information out of you. No one wants to work hard in casual conversation. That'll be easy enough if you follow Rule Number 3.

Rule Number 3: **Be prepared to talk about yourself and your work.** That awful moment: someone asks you about the new play you're writing and what you describe sounds like a bad rerun of *Dallas* written under the influence of mind-altering drugs. I always hated that question "What's your new play about?" until I finally realized I was always unprepared to answer it. And because I was unprepared and couldn't collect my thoughts quickly enough, I would end up butchering the story. Then I'd feel bad, they'd have a look of feigned interest on their face, and we'd both mumble and stumble our way to another topic of conversation. But the real danger here is this: if I sound confused about my play, what kind of impression am I evoking for my listener?

Just as you'll have to learn to write a synopsis of your play, you have to be able to condense the story even more, to three or four cogent sentences that you can offer up when someone asks the dreaded question. The formula for this should be not unlike what our friends in Hollywood use: the pitch. Give it a genre, give it a verb, give it some action, and give it a conclusion.

> It's a dark comedy about a bitter New York playwright who's going blind and hires a southern woman to help him transcribe his last play, and through their relationship his life and writing changes—but is it for the better?

If your listener's interested in your pitch, they'll ask more questions about your play. Be prepared to answer them. And don't be afraid to answer a question with, "I don't know, I haven't thought about that yet." They'll appreciate your candor. Have something like this for every play you've written in case they ask, "What else have you written?" Then let Rule Number 4 kick in.

Rule Number 4: **Be excited about your work.** If you're not excited about your work, why would anyone else be? But being excited about your work implies liking your work and seeing the value in what you've written. It means that you don't routinely apologize for it or its shortcomings, or dismiss every reading, showcase production, or fully mounted production of your work because it wasn't at a regional theatre. It means you don't make a bellyload of excuses for why you haven't written more, better, faster, or funnier. It means you don't blame someone else for your lack of enjoyment about your writing. Be your own cheerleader—but don't be obnoxious about it. Invite your listener to enjoy your joy. What could be so bad about that?

The Golden Moment. They say, "I'd like to read your play." Be cool. Relax. Breathe. Thank them. Even thank them again. Not a third time, though. Tell them you'll get your play right to them and at their convenience. Make it easy for them. So easy they'll hardly know it's under their nose when they look down. But don't promise them something you can't give them. Don't tell them you'll get it to them within the hour/day/week if you can't. Don't tell them you've finished a draft of the play when you've only written the first eight pages. Be honest. Make yo' mama proud, and *just be honest.* It might feel like an opportunity slipping away, but no more so than when you've burned that bridge because you couldn't deliver what you said you could.

Alright, final moments. Shake hands. That's right. Touch them. Literally. People remember things like human contact. But don't be a jerk and give them the cold fish for a handshake. Shake their hand like you're already signing a deal. *Fake* your security if you have to. Smile at them. Let them know you've really enjoyed the talk. Then go home and get to work delivering what you've promised.

My first agent, a real slick guy half my age at the William Morris Agency, gave me this savvy advice: "Make yourself into a friggin' Christmas tree that everybody wants to hang a ball on." At the time, I didn't know what the hell he was talking about. Now I do. No one's going to promote you like you should promote yourself. It's hard. I know it's hard. Believe it or not, I'm painfully shy around people I don't know. I've got issues about how I look, how I talk, how talented I really am, how interesting my work really is. But I get nowhere if what you remember most about me is my insecurity.

A *Treatise on Kissing Ass.* I guess we should talk about it. If it was bad enough for Mama Rose ("Have an eggroll, Mr. Goldstone . . ."), I guess it's bad enough for us. What am I going to say? Don't do it? You're going to do it. We all do it. We won't admit to it, but we all do it. We're practically conditioned to do it around people in authority or in power. They're part of the problem. They like it. And if they're egomaniacs (and in the theatre you can guess what the chances of that are), they like a lot of it. I was never much for it, but believe me, I've slipped here and there. I guess as you get older you realize you don't like to kiss something that doesn't kiss back. It doesn't feel good. But if you're going to do it, be smart about it. Know who's watching you, and know how many times they've seen you do it. Don't become known as the playwright with the big lips.

* * *

FOR YOUR SOUL

(This is the stuff you should think about when you can't write and
you're trying to figure out why.)

* * *

Spandex, My Bicep, and Writer's Block

This is my theory on writer's block: I'm hurt and I don't want to be hurt again, so I avoid writing like I avoid going to the gym. When the planets, moons, comets, black holes, and the NASA space shuttle are in perfect alignment, I go to one of those fancy, state-of-the-art "look!-there's-Keanu Reeves-what's-he-doing-in-my-gym?" gym, three, four, maybe even five times a week. Not because, God knows, I don't have anything better to do. And not because I think that with hours of sweat, pain, and exhaustion (and all that manly man grunting, moaning, and screaming), I can look like 85 percent of the people around me (although I've developed a helluva bicep).

I go to the gym because I turned forty-two this year, and (1) I'm vain—my mid-section looks like it's incubating a large, bulbous alien child, and as Kevin, my trainer, has often said, "Spandex is a privilege, not a right"; (2) I'm scared—I have an irregular heartbeat from drinking too much coffee (I've been told), and my cardiologist says that exercise strengthens the heart muscle; and (3) I've been trying to stop smoking for the last twelve years and have somehow fooled myself into believing that strenuous exercise cancels out the ill effects of smoking. What a crock.

Here's the sad reality: I can have what I want. I can look like a Calvin Klein magazine ad in a heartbeat if I do one simple set of aerobic exercises for thirty minutes three times a week. With a little bit of effort, I could wear my spandex proudly and finally shed myself of the four layers of clothing I wear now. I can stop looking at other bodies thinking they have a secret I don't know about, or they're God given, or inherited, or negotiated through the devil. All I have to do is throw on those running shorts, step in to my beat-up Nikes, trot down to the exercise room, and let Gloria Estefan sing me into a rapturous sweat.

But you couldn't pay me to do it. Why? I'm scared. I have a bad knee, a weak ankle, and I'm afraid of getting hurt. It's not rational. I was injured a long time ago. Yeah, alright, every once in a while I might feel a twinge in my ankle or a tightness in my knee, but nothing that makes me immobile or even uncomfortable. But I can't seem to shake the feeling of fear and expectation that my effort will lead me back to an injury that is physiologically central to my mobility. If I can't move, where can I go? If I can't walk, what will I do? So I stand at the glass window, looking in at all the "beautiful people" getting more beautiful, filled with self-loathing for not having the courage to transcend my fears and take the first steps.

I think we experience the same phenomenon as playwrights. God knows I do. I can remember every negative criticism that's ever been leveled at my work. I can remember every friend that's walked away from a reading of my play without saying anything. I can remember phone calls that weren't made to discuss my play or the look on people's faces as they can't think of what to say after seeing my play in production. In an instant, I can conjure up the names of all those agents and agencies that never responded to my submissions, or hear the curt response from a literary manager I called to discover the whereabouts of my play.

YES, I'M SENSITIVE. I ADMIT IT! I am a well of raw feelings: But that's part of the reason I'm a good writer. My feelings are right in front of me. My heart is everywhere for anyone to see. My soul twists and turns itself inside out to respond to a monstrously delicate balance of life and love. So, yeah, I remember the pain and heartache. Of course, I can relive my injuries time and again. Here's the rub: the pain that makes me an interesting writer is the same pain that keeps me from writing. Just as my knee injury keeps me from sweating my way to a size 32 waistline, my injuries in the theatre keep me from getting close to my keyboard.

Do you recognize any of this? You don't want to start a new play because nothing happened to the last three you wrote, and on some profound level, that hurts. You don't want to begin act 2 of your new play because that's where things broke down during the reading of your last play and *everybody* was vocal about it, and that hurts. You don't want to write that character who is incredibly complex because somebody remarked how shallow the characters in your last play were, and that hurt. You can't write the dialogue to a pivotal scene because some insensitive friend made a joke out of some dialogue you wrote for a play ten years ago. And on and on and on.

Or how about this? You write a play that everyone heralds as the greatest play of the decade. Everyone says this is the play that will make your career; this is the play that will get you into every major regional theatre in the country; this play will get you an agent, a production, a relationship with a literary manager, the Julie Harris Award for Playwriting, or a contract with a major Hollywood film company and fought over by movie stars. And then the silence is deafening. Nothing happens. No calls. No offers. No agents trying to outdo each other for your attention. And you're left to answer your die-hard supporters' questions with an embarrassed, "I don't know what happened." You think: what the hell am I doing this for? If I write the best thing that I can, and nothing happens, why do I keep writing? And that's a big injury.

Maybe this is your story: you've defied conventional wisdom. You didn't go to business school. You looked your mom, dad, girlfriend, or boyfriend square in the eye and said, "I'm a writer. I want to be a playwright." And after they tried to convince you that there is no money, no future, no *anything* associated with the theatre and you defended your choice as if your life depended on it (and maybe it does), you're left to prove something to these people who doubted your choice from the start. So it's you and them. It's your dream versus theirs. And it sets you up to have to prove to them that they're wrong. Every opportunity in the theatre becomes a chance to prove you were right. And if you don't succeed quickly (and who does in the theatre?), the injury begins to fester.

How do we get beyond all of this? How can we write despite cumulative injuries of our careers-in-process? I know this is easier said than done, but you've got to knock the injuries down until no hurt is left standing. I'm a firm believer in it's never too late to right a wrong. Call your friend or teacher who avoided you after the reading of your play and say, "You know what? You never said a word about my play, *and that feels lousy.*" Talk to your parents or companion. Say this out loud: "I need your support. I know you don't think this is the right thing for me to do, but I need you with me, not against me. It's a lonely sport I'm playing, so I need as many people in the grandstand as I can get." Write

29

a second letter to all of those agents and agencies that never responded to you. Say to them, "I never received a response to my letter of inquiry, and as I'm still seeking representation, I thought you might advise me on how best to get a response."

If you do what I suggest, you may get a positive response. Then again, you may get no response. But one thing I know for sure: we have to take care of ourselves and we have to take action—it's no one else's responsibility. And that means we have to educate people about how to treat us as playwrights. If we don't, we won't survive our careers. We'll stop writing and blame everyone but ourselves or, worse, blame only ourselves. So talk! Let everyone know what you need. Call people on their bad behavior. What, you'd rather sit there and feel bad about yourself than tell your insensitive lout of a friend that falling asleep during the production of your play is not cool by you?

We can't expect anyone to intuit our world or our feelings. We have to share our world, fears, doubts, insecurities. There's no book that tells your parents or friends what you need as an artist or how to behave around you. *You* have to tell them. You have to gather all the strength you can find and say to whomever, "After a reading, I'm really vulnerable, so what I need from you at the moment is your support, not your criticism." You have to be strong and stop your friend at the elevator and say, "You read my play, and you're avoiding me. You can not like my play and we can still be friends. But you can't stop talking to me." You have to take responsibility for a situation that could injure you because no one knows what you need more than you do.

Will this take away the pain, the injury? No, but maybe it'll lessen it just enough to get you back to the keyboard. Maybe it will make you feel better that you've done something about your injury instead of just hurting about it. Then make a promise to yourself that in the future, you'll address the hurt and injury at the moment it comes. When someone hurts you, be a lion in sheep's clothing. Nothing wrong with that.

Just got back from the gym. Took my first aerobics class. No Gloria Estefan, just some East Village house music. Felt like an idiot. Sweated my guts out. Didn't hurt my leg or my ankle. Going back tomorrow. Spandex never felt so good. Kevin's going to be so proud of me.

The Ties That Bind Us:
Mother, Mentor, Father, Teacher

North Junior High School's trend-setting production of *Miss Hepplewhite Takes Over*—a one-act play with not even the hint of a curse word, no political, social, or religious issues to explore, and full of stereotypical "boy" roles and "girl" roles—marked my auspicious debut on the stage. I slaughtered the competition in the audition because I wanted to be the guy who got to sneeze in a bowl of flour while making a cake—to my mind, the only moment in the play worth watching. I fantasized every day in rehearsal about the guaranteed gales of laughter that would flow from the audience when my big moment came. Mrs. Middleton, my drama teacher, never let me rehearse the bit because of the mess I'd make on her new linoleum floor. So I always mimed it during rehearsal. Big mistake.

When the big moment came in production, I practically inhaled the scenery to get enough air to blow a good sneeze. I popped the sneeze right into the bowl of flour, blew flour everywhere (big laughter from the audience), sucked some flour up my nose and down my throat, choked, and fainted. The curtain came down to thunderous applause. I was revived by a hysterical Mrs. Middleton, who, in between looks of intense concern, was trying to keep from laughing. Groggy and disoriented, I had enough consciousness to see her looking down at me and hear her saying, "That was the funniest thing I've ever seen." She went on to say something else that had phrases like "overdoing it," "mugging," and "safety" attached to it, but I wasn't listening. I was still on the phrase, "That was the funniest thing . . ." and I was hooked. That one little bit of encouragement was all I needed to begin a career.

As writers, all kinds of people encourage us along the way: mamas who defend our career choice to daddies; high school English writing teachers who praise our short stories and say warm words around us like "talented," "promising," and "gifted"; best friends who read every word we write and are outrageously supportive or outrageously critical; our first playwriting teacher who's firm, tough, hard, demanding, and insistent and who pushes us to write better than we ever thought possible; a boyfriend or girlfriend who's prouder than we are of our smallest accomplishment.

Our relationships with these people—who are everything to us, from the folks who literally teach us how to write in the classroom to those who gently encourage us to keep writing and not give up—are so complicated, so full of us, so full of them, and so emotionally charged it's a wonder we don't short out all the electrical appliances within a two-mile radius. We expect them, our supporters and "encouragers," to be superhuman: always available, always eager to hear and understand our frustrations with our writing, always ready to read our next draft. We tap these folks for their guidance, knowledge, advice, support, wisdom, caring heart, receptive ear, shoulder to cry on, or hand to hold. And more times than often, we expect them to be mind-readers and to know what we need, when we need it, and why.

We're like newborns, reliant on them for everything; happy when they protect us from the world and full of rage when they push us into it. We want them to love everything we write and are devastated when they don't. We empower them with mythic qualities, cowering when we think we've disappointed them or radiating when we've pleased them. We expect more of them than anyone else in our lives, and if they're our teachers, mentors, or instructors, *we expect even more than that*. Straight up: that's not fair.

Instructors, mentors, and teachers, no matter how informal or formal your arrangement with them, are human beings who can be all the wonderful things you expect them to be *and* be moody, inconsistent, fickle, angry, frustrated, tired, unfocused, and unwilling to coddle you. I know what I'm talking about. As a student I've been on the receiving end of it; as a teacher, I've delivered it. Having taught for almost twenty years now and despite my best intentions, I make wrong choices and big mistakes that sometimes involve my students. I wish that weren't so, but I have to own up to being human and, therefore, imperfect. It has taken me a long time and loads of heartache to realize that teachers are people, too.

I barely knew who I was as a person, let alone an artist, when I stumbled into the office of my very first playwriting teacher and asked to sign up for a playwriting class. Moments after I met him, I knew that he knew the world I wanted to see. Time proved me right. This was the man who finally held the mirror up for me to see who I was, who cleared years of garbage and confusion out of my mind and opened up channels of creativity in me that no other force or stimuli had succeeded in doing. He became my Savior from myself, my Defender of my choice to be a writer, my Provider of insights into the real life of a writer, my Spiritual Leader through the abyss this career can often be. I never considered for a moment that, by virtue of his position at the university, he had to be all of those things to thirty *other* people who felt the identical way I did. He had thirty needy children (students); I was only one more with my hand up, waving and shouting: "ME! ME!"

When I got out of school, we kept in contact. I'd ask him to read drafts of plays, invite him to my play readings, get him to talk about the theatre and share his wisdom (or at the very least, a contact or two). I began anchoring so many of my actions to his opinion that I practically lost sight of my own. I listened to every sage word of advice he could give me, reveled in his attention, and flourished under his tutelage. And then came what I now know is an almost inevitable period of cooling down and growing apart that an artist often experiences with an artistic parent.

Was it my imagination, or was he asking less and less about my writing? Did he actually flinch when I asked him to read the next draft of my new play, or did I just think he did? Were his comments about the production of my play really dismissive, or just not what I wanted to hear? There was nothing tangible ever said; no hints or pointed conversation that suggested I find wings because the time had come to fly out of the nest. It was very subtle . . . and decimating.

I felt his absence in my life, and every insecurity I had as a writer began to surface. The longer it went on, the more paranoid I became and believed that his behavior was purposeful, intended to do exactly what it was doing: creating a distance between him and me. I felt like he had fallen out of love with me but had forgotten to tell me. And like any spurned lover, I got depressed—so depressed I stopped writing. Completely. Couldn't get near the keyboard.

Why didn't I ever stop and just ask if there was a problem? Wouldn't that have been the easier thing to do than suffer all the personal drama that developed instead? On an intellectual level, talking about the problem would have been infinitely easier; on an emotional level, talking would have been impossible. My insecurities had consumed me, and I assumed there was only one reason for his behavior: he was losing interest in me because I was a lousy writer.

More damaging than anything else (in hindsight, of course) was the complete surrender of my power to this gentleman. I gave it away without knowing, completely innocent of what I was giving up and how it would drastically alter our relationship. Seduced into submission by his obvious knowledge and my assumed lack thereof, I infused him with every ounce of my own security about my talent and relied solely on him to judge my work and life as a writer for me. If I was a good writer, it was because he said I was a good writer. If my play was good or bad, it was because he told me it was and I believed him. How fair was that to him or me? Not fair at all, particularly because he was unaware of his power over me.

Only after becoming a playwriting teacher myself at NYU have I begun to understand what might have happened in the relationship with my first teacher. It's possible as the child in the relationship, and on some subconscious level, I wanted to pull away from my "artistic parent" and didn't have the courage to do it so I behaved in such a way as to force *him* to do it. Or perhaps, like any teacher or mentor, he had only so much energy to give out to other people before he bankrupted himself emotionally, and the more I pushed, the less he responded. There's a good chance I just made a nuisance of myself and wasn't terribly sensitive to his needs. Maybe, as a writer himself, he resented the time he was forced to give to me and his other students. It's possible he was frustrated with his own career, and perceived my burgeoning career as a threat on some level. Maybe he expected to be done with me when I graduated, but I kept reappearing, asking for more.

34

It's hard to know what happened. But I do know this: I've repeated the mistake I made with him many times since. I've given my power over to friends, family, other teachers, and most dangerously, to agents. I've allowed them to define my success or failure, haphazardly guide my career, and thoroughly confuse me by repelling their criticism and sucking in their praise with equal abandon. When I'm that vulnerable and open to anybody's suggestion at the blink of an eye, I surrender my good sense of self-direction and preservation.

Don't do it. Stop it while you can. Check in with those people who are your supporters and "encouragers." Ask them if they're OK with the attention you demand from them. And whatever you do, *don't relinquish your power to anybody*. Don't give it away, as I did, because I needed to be liked and loved and cared for and respected as a writer to the degree that I lost myself in the relationship. And if you already have a problem with a relationship, talk about it now.

I have to end this now. I'm taking the first step in my own recovery. I'm calling my first playwriting teacher to tell him I think I finally understand something I've been meaning to share with him.

I've Been to the Dark Side
(And Now I Want the Light)

I have no evidence to prove this, but I'd almost lay my life on the line that my mother was the distinguished philosopher who coined the adage "When life give you a lemon, make lemonade." I certainly heard her say it enough. This pearl of wisdom was a domestic tattoo in every house in our neighborhood—printed on calendars, embroidered on pillows, appliqued on the occasional sweatshirt, T-shirt, work shirt, or apron, or torn from the pages of *Redbook*, put in a K-Mart frame, and smartly hung in some place of prominence.

Over the years, anytime I've heard or seen that obnoxious ditty, it has made me want to smack someone. How dare anyone suggest that I actually choose to think positive when feeling negative feels so much better, so much richer, so much more dramatic. Being a dramatist, wouldn't it make sense to wrap myself in blankets of "I'm no good," "I'm not as good as . . ." or "If only I were . . ."? To me, feeling "less than" has always been a perfect fit; anything else would be like slipping on my father's size 42 boxer shorts.

In 1997, I was given a gift: my two best friends from college happened to be working in New York at the same time as me. This chance occurrence was the first time in ten years, since leaving the University of Michigan, that we crossed paths for any length of time. That was the good news.

The bad news: how I discovered they were there. One Sunday in early August, I opened up the "Arts & Leisure" section of the *New York Times* to find one of my friends, Douglas Sills, highlighted in a photograph and full-page feature article about his good fortune in landing a starring role in the Broadway production of *The Scarlet Pimpernel*—Douglas was the Scarlet Pimpernel. On the previous page (I kid you not) was a half-page picture of my other college friend, Tim Hopper, and an article about his arrival at New York Theatre Workshop in a controversial production of O'Neill's *More Stately Mansions.* Thank God I live just on the second floor of my building.

Was I proud of them? Of course, incredibly proud. Was I excited that these two extraordinary actors would get all the praise they deserved? Absolutely. Both these guys are destined for huge careers in the theatre. But was I green with jealousy? *Bright* green, luminescent green. I was so jealous of their success I could barely walk a straight line. After I spent the next couple of days chewing my insides out, thrashing my ego to within an inch of its fragile life, and vowing (à la Scarlett O'Hara) that "as God as my witness, I will never be 'less than' again," I had a good, quiet talk with myself.

So many of us think success is measured with a yardstick that has a Broadway production at the top, an off-Broadway production three-quarters of the way up, a regional production at the halfway mark, and an agent who loves our work a quarter of the way up. Anything else in our lives that has to do with our writing hardly registers at the bottom of the stick (or isn't even there for the measuring). I don't know about you, but I say it's high time we break that stick in half and toss it away, because who knows what's going to happen in life? I want to be able to look back and embrace every opportunity I've had in a theatre with the happiness and joy it gave me—as opposed to what it could or should have been—don't you?

As a playwright, redefining success for myself has now become an absolute necessity. I've already done everything else. I've sat and quietly loathed the playwright in my writing group who just got an agent. I've raged in a fury when a writer who I know isn't as talented as I am got a grant, fellowship, or production. I've trashed the most recent opening of a Broadway play and filled a conversation with grand statements like "How can he write that garbage and get away with it?" In my head, I've publicly heckled the Pulitzer committee and jeered the Tony committee. I've refused to read the "Arts & Leisure" section of the *New York Times* and vehemently disagreed with every critic in print over the past ten years. I've ignored the solicitations for new plays in the *Dramatists*

Guild Newsletter and the *Dramatists Sourcebook* because, really, what's the point? Sadly, I've also minimized my own efforts, because it didn't fit my bloated definition of success.

Enough. I'm done. I've been to the Dark Side—and it ain't pretty. It's time for a change—a big change—that will become my new domestic tattoo.

For all of us who don't have a contract with a regional theatre or a production on Broadway next year (all 99.9 percent of us), I'll redefine our success to include:

1. Writing a play we've been meaning to write for years but haven't because we were (a) too unsure of our talent, (b) too distant from our hearts, (c) too distant from our passion, (d) too aware of what we thought agents, theatres, and literary managers wanted to see. To begin something new that's been asleep in your brain for the past five years is a *successful step forward*.

2. Finishing a full draft of that play (even if it takes the whole year), or the first act, or the first scene, or the character biographies. Just fleshing out the idea on paper will be *worth celebrating*, because it's no longer just a nagging idea that hasn't been given the privilege of exploration.

3. Having a reading of a scene, an act, a first draft. In our redefinition, we will also agree that, no, Steppenwolf doesn't have to do the reading. No, it doesn't have to be with Equity actors. No, it doesn't have to meet with unanimous praise. No, it doesn't have to be a brilliant read. Yes, it can have flaws. Yes, it can need a complete rewrite and still qualify as a success, because we've finally stopped protecting the idea of a play that we didn't think we could write and exposed our strengths and weaknesses as an artist—something that takes enormous courage.

4. Making theatre friends and finding a theatre home. Baby, it's paradise when we find a group of actors or a director or a managing producer of a theatre who looks at us and says "I like your work. Can I see something else of yours?" Send the

fireworks up. *Celebrate.* For a drama jock, there's no place like a playing field you can call home. If we know a group of people who eagerly await our next play (think of Lanford Wilson and the Circle Rep, Terrence McNally and the Manhattan Theatre Club), imagine the possibilities for our creative souls. Yeah, it'd be nice if it was Actors Theatre of Louisville, but if it's five friends and a futon, something good can come of it.

5. Overcoming the discouragement. Whew! How do we do that? I don't know, but if I achieved numbers 1 through 4 above, maybe I'd forget my past disappointments. That's not true. I wouldn't forget, but maybe I wouldn't remember them so vividly—and that's big-time success.

And if we can't find the time, guts, courage, or energy to write a new play, we'll honor these successes of an old play:

1. We'll recognize that five out of the ten rejection letters we received have been more positive than negative, or,

   a. We'll recognize that a literary manager actually took the time to write a rejection letter that's not a form letter, or,

   b. We'll recognize that we got a personal call from the literary manager saying that although the theatre's not going forward with the play, she did like it and thinks it's very well written. *"Wait a minute!" you say. "Yes, they wrote a nice letter or made a call, but they're still not doing my play!" Well . . . how many other playwrights didn't get a letter or a phone call? Hmm? I assure you: hundreds.* We have to count small successes to survive the big disappointments.

2. A community theatre does a reading of your play. Yeah, it's not the Mark Taper, it's not even Theatre by the Bakery, but it's a reading nonetheless, and you'll learn something about your play.

3. Someone walks up to you after the reading of your play and says, "You don't know me, but I just wanted to tell you how much I enjoyed your play" or "I've never laughed so hard . . ." or "I didn't know anyone else understood the way I feel." Do

we shrug these comments off because they're not from Big Broadway Producers? No!

4. A friend introduces you to someone as a talented writer.
5. Two successes: Your mother, father, sister, brother, or companion asks what you're writing; and you have a lucid response. That family thing can shake anyone to their core, and if you have family that is actually *interested* in what you're doing, answer their questions and include them in your professional life. It's a win-win thing.
6. Your mother, father, sister, brother, or companion asks to read your play and you actually give it to them.
7. Your mother, father, sister, brother, or companion likes your play and can even talk about it in a way that you can hear it.
8. An actor seeks you out to say he loved your writing, and you take his phone number because who knows when you'll need an actor for a reading.
9. A director tells you she'd really like to get her hands on one of your plays, and you take her address and phone number and periodically give her a call to stay in touch.
10. You get a production of your play in some small theatre that is genuinely proud to be presenting your work. What a wonder it is to see all these people work like dogs because they think *you* have something interesting to say.
11. You get a review in a local newspaper that mentions the writing.
12. You're proud of yourself at the end of the day.

Am I oversimplifying? Maybe. But I can now. I've done too much of the other, and it does nothing but make me angrier, more jaded, more cryptic, and frankly, less appealing to be around. Life is too short, and this profession too fickle, for me not to see the smallest success as a giant gift.

Tina Turner, Lanford Wilson, and Me

I worship Tina Turner. Who wouldn't? Beautiful, sexy, ageless, sassy, talented, bold, brash, spirited, rebellious, courageous, and a survivor of her past. I wish I had a nickel for every time I've thrown caution to the wind, turned on my CD player, cranked up the volume well above the comfort level, and blasted "What's Love Got To Do With It" for the rest of Manhattan to hear. The visuals alone are worth the price of admission: Tina screaming in the background while I'm dusting/vacuuming/folding sheets/scrubbing the bathtub, with my ass swaying to the beat. At some point when the music takes me over, I'll grab a bottle of Suave shampoo or my feather duster, tilt my head back, and belt out the high note on my makeshift microphone. You can't tell me we aren't cut from the same cloth.

Miss Tina's music sends me somewhere. There's a steady, rhythmic beat, a story to tell, her feelings thrown all over the notes, a gravelly, gritty tone in her voice, and a fearlessness that speaks to years of having "been there, done that, and survived—with intense therapy." In the simplest way of thinking, she's got a compelling story to tell and learned over the years how to tell it and make me appreciate not only her talent but her courage for saying what's on her mind.

Tina's my kind of hero. She consistently rocks my soul, takes me away from my darkest self, and elevates my spirit from its quagmire. Tina spills her guts out for me to see, collapses in an emotional heap, picks herself back up, brushes herself off, and then smiles a cocky smile as if to say, "Now, that wasn't so bad, was it?" Yeah, that's my kind of hero. And I need a hero. We all do, don't we?

As playwrights, it may seem odd to think we should look for a hero in the theatre, but I think it's something we desperately need—someone to look up to, to emulate, to aspire to, to try to copy, for God's sake. We need to know a living playwright's intimate history, discover her humble roots, learn how she worked her way forward in her career, beat the odds, survived, and flourished. We need to read her words of wisdom, caution, and advice and absorb ourselves in her life lessons.

But I see most of us rebel against that idea, as if to suggest that we'll lose our own unique voice if we emulate someone else. It can't happen. You are you. You will never be William Shakespeare, Molière, Marie Irene Fornes, or Henry David Hwang. You've got a creative fingerprint that no one can copy, so why not immerse yourself in the glorious work of others? There's so much to learn there. And I'm not talking just about reading plays. I'm suggesting that we each find a role model and get to know the whole of them. Therein lies our education.

When I was in graduate school rebelling against all things academic, the thought of doing a master's thesis and doctoral dissertation was enough to make me pull out what little hair I had left. I futzed around for months on end, trying to figure out something that wouldn't put me to sleep while writing it. For my master's thesis, I finally settled on something like "An Examination of the Comedic Technique of Neil Simon." For my doctoral dissertation, it was "Lanford Wilson's Use of Comedy and Humor." If nothing else, I'd get a couple of good yuks out of the process while doing my research and reading their work.

When I began my research on Simon, I was much more interested in the idea of "what is comedy, what is humor" than I was on anything about Neil Simon. I mean, yeah, Simon was a playwright who wrote comedies and was more successful at it than anyone in contemporary theatre. But I could have cared less about that. I just wanted to know how he did it. I wanted the formula—the magic equation. I wanted his rule book, so that I could use the good stuff and ditch the bad. Needless to say, I wasn't prepared to discover that a writer and his work are inextricable—and to understand a person's art means, on some level, understanding the person.

Studying Simon, I learned how enriched as an artist I could become by thoroughly examining another's creative and personal life. How could I not learn from Simon's struggles, failures, successes? How could I not appreciate his drive and ambition? How could I not read or see any plays he'd written and not understand the grueling process the play underwent before I became privy to it? It taught me a lesson, a *big* lesson I've never forgotten: know yourself in art, but *know a few others along the way*. It helps.

When I went on to get a Ph.D., Lanford Wilson was my theatre god. The man could do no wrong. For me, his plays were the ultimate theatre experience, full of humor, pathos, rich characterizations, interesting ideas, daring structures, poetry, exacting dialogue, and wit. I read everything of his I could get my hands on. I read every article that detailed his growth as a writer. I knew his background, his journey to New York City, his first work at Café Cino, his historical move to create Circle Rep, his triumphs there, his awards, his moves to Broadway, and his failures. I knew him on paper almost as well as anybody I knew in person . . . and then I met him.

Not far from the old Circle Repertory Theatre Company in Sheridan Square in New York City was an old hangout, a bar and restaurant called The Lion's Den. Smoky, crowded, noisy, full of artists and blue-collar folks—heaven. I was in New York City to finish up the research on my dissertation, and found myself at a place a friend thought would be great fun for dinner—The Lion's Den. I walked in and, like a scene from a movie, he was sitting at the bar just inside the door. I recognized him immediately. I was stunned. This was the first real famous person I'd ever seen, and it was somebody I knew intimately who didn't know I even existed. In two seconds, I managed to maneuver my way to the bar right beside him and just stared, completely star-struck.

Frozen at first by a thousand thoughts rushing in my head at the same time, I finally broke free of my paralysis, (I can't believe I did this) pulled my dissertation out of my book bag, and plopped all 259 pages right onto the bar. I don't know why I did it; it just seemed right. Worse, I began flipping casually through it, hoping he'd spot his name and ask me about it. No such luck. He kept talking to his friend (another playwright, Jim Leonard), laughing and smoking.

I asked that he pass me an ashtray. He did. I asked that he pass me some matches. He did. I asked that he give me a cigarette (where did I get the courage?). He did, looked at me, and said, "And do you want me to smoke that for you?" Without blinking, I said, "No, but I would like you to autograph this book that I've just written about you." What followed was the most intense ten minutes of my life to that point. Not only did he autograph the manuscript, he also read a few pages and made some corrections (!). When my friend walked in (and picked up her jaw from the floor), I thanked him and dashed away. I don't remember much after walking away from him because I had met my hero. My friend and I spent the rest of the night in an altered state of reality.

A year later in the Playwrights Lab at Circle Rep, I was sitting surrounded by some of the theatre's most prestigious theatre people and learning how to be a better playwright from the Best of the Best: Lanford, Lanie Robertson, Bill Hoffman, Milan Stitt, Tanya Berezin, John Bishop, Marshall Mason. That same year, I began working at NYU and saw these folks every day of the week in my own department. I felt lucky then, and I feel lucky now. The thrill of being around writers who've done it, who've made the grade, is something I will always crave no matter how old I get. I need them in front of me, to show me the way, to give me hope, guidance, and the courage to persevere. I need to learn from their mistakes and applaud their triumphs. I need to look up to someone, to believe there's a place for me among their ranks and a reason to work as hard as I do. I need a hero.

Flush It (An Internal Monologue)

You desperately try to ignore it, but that computer or typewriter sitting on your makeshift writer's table is like a two-ton elephant sitting in your living room and staring back at you. It's got eyes that follow you everywhere. You won't, can't, go near it. You force yourself not to think about it. You walk out of the room so you don't have to look at it. Seconds later, you're back in the room, staring it down. Impulsively, you sit, crack your knuckles, and prepare to create.

Now you've been sitting there for hours. Nothing's coming. Same thing happened yesterday, and the day before that. You're getting more and more despondent. You feel like you'll never write again. Your mind's blank—not a creative impulse anywhere. You think if you work on an old draft of a play it'll jump-start your imagination. You look at the old play. Nothing. You feel worse. You go back to a blank page to start something new. Nothing. You flip back to the old play. Nothing again. You call a friend to feel better. He makes you feel worse. Nothing's working. Desperate times call for desperate measures, so you smoke another pack of cigarettes. Now you feel sick. You eat another pizza. You feel worse. STOP!!!

Grab a pencil, rip these pages out (or xerox them), check into what you're really feeling, and check it *off*.

- ☐ I'm too old to be writing. They're only doing plays by eighteen-year-olds anyway.
- ☐ I'm _____ (fill in the blank). They're only doing plays by African Americans, women, gay people, or the physically challenged anyway.
- ☐ Most theatres are only doing new plays by known playwrights.
- ☐ I never studied playwriting. If I didn't study it, there's no way I can really do it.

☐ I've never had anything produced so I can't present myself as a writer.

☐ I don't even have an agent. No theatre will take me seriously.

☐ Professor _____ (fill in the blank) implied I was a lousy writer. And he's right. Never mind that I disagree with him on just about everything else. With this, he's right.

☐ I never heard back from the Theatre in a Tent, and they're a small theatre, so why bother? God, if I can't even get *them* to look at my work . . .

☐ I don't have enough money to mail my work out once I've finished it, so what's the point?

☐ I don't have a printer cartridge or paper for my computer, or a print ribbon for my typewriter.

☐ I hate rewriting.

☐ I never finish anything.

☐ I had such a bad reading of this play, it's not worth working on it.

☐ No one liked my last play, so what's the use of writing another?

☐ All I write is one-acts anyway, and no one's producing one-acts.

☐ My mother called and asked when I was going to take life seriously and get a real job instead of waiting tables so I'm free to write.

☐ My boyfriend/best friend called and said that he hopes that this play doesn't get any interest because then I'll be in rehearsal and he hates it when I spend that much time away from him.

☐ No one will ever produce this play because the issue of _____ (fill in the blank with anything you are currently writing about). That subject is ☐ overwritten ☐ too dark ☐ too controversial ☐ too embarrassing for my parents to know I've written about ☐ in need of too much research before I write ☐ already written better in *Angels in America*.

☐ I don't really like the theatre anyway.

☐ Nobody can make a living in the theatre.

☐ I'd rather write a screenplay.

☐ I'm better at writing poetry, fiction, essays, term papers, or short stories.

☐ The only director I know did a bad reading of my last play, so who could I get to direct another reading of anything I write?

☐ Everyone liked my last play so much, how can I top that?

☐ My heart's been broken recently, so I'm afraid it'll spill out onto my pages.

☐ _____ (fill in the blank).

☐ _____ (one more time; you've got plenty, I'm sure).

OK. You've identified why you can't get anywhere in your writing or won't even go near your computer or typewriter. Now wad this up and go flush it in the toilet. These are weak excuses that keep you from doing what you're meant to do. Writing's hard. Rewriting's harder. Submitting your plays out into the universe is a nightmare. But you're a playwright, damn it. It's what you have to do to be heard by as many people as possible. Stop with the excuses. Now, go to work.

PART 2

*Genuine beginnings begin with us, even when they
are brought to our attention by external opportunities.*

William Bridges

* * *

FOR YOUR HEAD

(Let's get down and get dirty. This is the real "nuts and bolts" stuff
that can make you a better playwright or prepare you
for a life in the theatre.)

* * *

Who Are All These People and
What Are They Doing to My Play?

No matter what your experience is in the theatre, the moment will come when you sit in an audience to watch a production of your play . . . and not recognize what you've written. It has happened to all of us at one time or another. My first New York production was a one-act I'd written straight out of college, *The Big, Fat, Naked Truth*. I thought I was being very theatre savvy by writing a play for five women (translate: five good parts for actresses), no set (a single folding chair and three walls painted some variation on white), and three props (a switchblade, a textbook, and a piece of paper). Think *No Exit* meets *Steel Magnolias* and sideswipes *Uncommon Women and Others* and you'll start to get the idea of the play.

What I wrote was a very dark comedy. What I saw was . . . well, frankly, I don't know what I saw, but trust me, there was no comedy in sight. It sounded like the play I wrote—I mean, the actresses were saying the words I'd written. And sure enough, there were three walls, a folding chair, and the requisite hand props. But from the moment the first actress stepped on-stage and began talking, I knew something was very wrong—like the basic interpretation of her character. When the second actress hit the stage, things really began sliding downhill. By the time the fifth actress arrived, I had murder and suicide foremost on my mind. I looked at the director, who was thrilled with her own work and feverishly mouthing the words to my text, and who looked like a ventriloquist act gone horribly awry. God, it was painful. What could I do but learn for the next time?

If you're lucky, the answer to the question Who are all these people and what are they doing to my play? is they are a highly creative group of people who share the *same vision of your play* that you do and who enjoy the efforts of *collaboration*. We're talking about actors, directors, dramaturgs, costumers, set designers, lighting designers, sound designers, props masters, fight choreographers, stage managers, stagehands, public relations people, artistic directors—all those gloriously inspired and creative people who work toward the greater whole. Everyone involved with your play tirelessly conspires to translate your message to a public audience. You need to know everything you can about them, just as they certainly need to know all about you. Make it your responsibility. Take the initiative. You'll be much happier for doing that, and chances are you won't be watching a version of your play that looks like *Medea* meets *The Matchmaker*.

Actors

I'm not ashamed to admit it: I love actors! For all they have ever done for my work, I will worship at their feet. It's almost incomprehensible what an actor contributes to the development of a new play. I am a better, more honest writer because I've had the good fortune to work with actors who care about what I have to say and question how I say it. And I will always write for the theatre because a good actor can deliver intricacies of my imagination that can leave an audience, and me, breathless.

I often encounter playwrights who have little appreciation for what an actor brings to the experience of a new play. At the very least, a good actor understanding your text will fill in the unwritten emotional gaps either by stringing together emotional associations you've supplied in the text, or simply by inventing them on the fly. Insightful actors can tell you what's missing in the emotional life of your work because it is their job to bring honesty and logic to their characterizations. A skilled actor will speak your words effortlessly, and when she/he can't because of your writing, she/he'll craftily transpose the words to make it "right for the mouth." Actors question every word that doesn't feel right, struggle with characterizations that are thinly drawn, and challenge you to sharpen your intention so that it's clear to them and, therefore, to the audience. Embrace their questions, listen to their suggestions, observe their choices and intuition—it'll all serve to make a better play.

Actors need to talk to you, so prepare yourself. They need to understand the back story of the characters, why you wrote the play, what you're trying to say, why you chose to set it in Alaska, or why act 1 ends with a character revelation that isn't followed through in act 2. Why? Because while you have your butt seated comfortably in a chair and are hidden somewhere in the audience watching your play, actors are on stage, vulnerable and exposed in front of an entire audience. They don't want to look like idiots. They want to look like they know what they're doing, and sometimes you are the key. Too often I've seen that awkward moment in rehearsal when an actor asks the writer a question about why something happens in the text and is answered with a blank, "I don't know." Well, if you as the writer don't know, who does? It's your job to know, and if you genuinely don't know the answer, figure it out with your director or dramaturg because your actors need answers. You wrote it—but they're trying to act it with intelligence.

Actors have their own creative process (take an acting class if you're not familiar enough with it) that can be both fascinating and horrifying to you as a writer. In rehearsal, they'll take three steps toward the character you wrote and five steps back. They'll mangle your dialogue then make it crystal clear. They'll change intentions in a scene four or five times, none of which you conceived of. They'll reveal things about the character you never knew were there and bury some things that are best left buried. They'll make you doubt every word you've written and then celebrate every word. Their process is complicated, tumultuous, and fragile. And while you don't have to walk on eggshells around actors, you do have to be sensitive to their creative process. Here are a few ideas that may help:

1. If an actor asks you a question about something in the text, it's because—believe it or not, no matter how clear you think you've written it—the answer's not clear to them. It's not an insult, it's a question. Help them out. Answer the question as completely as you can because it has a direct influence on their performance. Also realize that when an actor asks you a question, the answer could be crystal clear in the text and the actor just wants to hear some affirmation of his/her own thinking. This is a way for an actor to "check-in" to his/her own growth in the process.

2. If an actor challenges you about something you've written—a line of dialogue, the intention behind a scene, or the purpose of an action a character takes, think about *why* they're asking what they're asking, and allow that to guide your answer. Perhaps the actor can't find the motivation to make the moment honest; perhaps the actor is uncomfortable with how the moment is structured, so the moment doesn't feel "earned" or the actor can't make the emotional connection to a memory or past event in the character's life. Actors are invaluable to the development of a new play because they operate from a place of sensitivity and intuition, and what they challenge you about is often a matter of logic that isn't honest to the character as they see it. Try to resolve their confusion so that they can make an emotional connection to the text. Be warned though: if you can't explain it clearly, don't expect the actor to play it clearly—the "garbage in, garbage out" theory. A second warning: if you find you're having to explain too much, one of two things is happening: either it's not clear in the text or the actor's being daft. Talk to your director if you need help figuring this out.

3. Actors will never give you 100 percent of the character you see in your head. They can't. They can't see inside of your head. Your job is to make the characterizations as richly detailed and textured in the text as possible so that the actor can illuminate your fantasy as you dramatically envision it. Think of it this way: if you describe a landscape you see in your head to a friend and ask him/her to draw it, the more detailed you are, the more accurate a picture your friend can draw of your vision. The less detailed you are, the more room there is for your friend to interpret.

4. At some point in the rehearsal process, the actor becomes an equal authority of the character you've written. They have to do this. They have to understand that character so completely that they can fabricate anything in the life of "Tony" or "Tina." You'll become aware of this phenomenon when you challenge a choice made by the actor and she/he

responds by saying, "Danny would never walk in the door with his hat on. He has too much respect for his mother and father and how he was raised." There doesn't have to be a battle of wills around this. Listen to what the actor is saying, and either agree or disagree by evincing how the character consistently behaves in the text that is written.

5. Line readings (or, telling an actor how to say a line you've written to make the most sense of it) is not your place. Don't do it. Resist it. Tape your mouth shut if you have to. Allow the actors to find their way. Chances are they'll come to the sense of it eventually in rehearsal. They need to make it organic for themselves, and you telling them the end result is not helpful. If the actors look like they'll never get there, talk to your director. See if there is something she/he can do to help the actors out. You'll never be more tempted to do this as when you've written a comedy and an actor's not getting the laugh you think is there. Again, talk to the director.

6. Don't give actors acting notes, even as seemingly innocent as, "You know, the character really should be more angry in that scene." That isn't your job. It's the director's. Anything you have to say about what an actor is doing on stage should be funneled through your director. Actors need to hear *one* voice and one direction to gain the security they need to be clear on stage. Your voice muddles it up.

7. Actors, like everyone, need approval. They're going to ask you what you think about how they're doing. This is dangerous territory, especially in rehearsal. Of course, if you're asked, you have to say something. But realize anything you say can have a profound effect on their work—after all, they want to please you. Show an actor you're disappointed in his/her work and watch the panic grow. Show an actor you're completely pleased with what she/he is doing and you run the risk of their complacency.

8. A word of sincere caution: you will be more than tempted to expect the same fabulous performance by your lead actor night after night after night. You will assume that, if any-

thing, your actor will only get better in each performance. Your actor, for the most part, believes and wants the same thing. But actors are not machines. They can't give you cookie-cutter perfection every night. Despite his best effort, your actor will blow a laugh line in the eighth performance that she/he nailed in the previous seven. Chalk it up to one thing—she/he's a human being—and allow his/her humanity. Frustrating as it may be, it is the nature of the beast in live performance.

9.   When all's said and done, if you're happy with what the actors have brought to the stage, praise them. Thank them. Support them. Let them know how much you appreciate their effort. Overdo it—it doesn't cost you anything. Make them want to work with you again. Actors are invaluable resources, and you need them as your allies in art.

Directors

It's a marriage. Ain't no two ways about it. You've got a wedding date, you've got all the people to make the wedding happen, and the challenge for the both of you is to find a way to make the "I do" sound like the Mormon Tabernacle Choir sang it. The right relationship with your director is *the* most critical element in the production of your play. You both have to be on the same page, seeing eye to eye, walking the same walk, and talking the same talk. The relationship you form can be a lifetime thing, and your creative collaboration can propel your play forward to a place you never dreamed of if you do two things: communicate and negotiate your relationship up front.

Communication doesn't seem like a terribly hard concept to grasp, but for some reason, a playwright all too often sits on feelings instead of sharing them with the person perceived to be in charge. I can't figure out why this happens, but I'm inclined to think that playwrights are worriers: we worry that we'll offend the director if we offer a suggestion or solution or question a choice; we worry that the director is already overburdened with so many other things to think about that the last thing she/he needs is to hear from us; we worry that we'll appear "precious" about our work if we question the director's interpretation; we worry that our own judgment isn't sound, so we defer to the director's judgment and opinion. We're afraid to infringe on the director's artistry, so we don't challenge a casting choice, a light cue, the placement of a set piece, or an actor's delivery of a line. And if the director really *loves our play*, all of the above is intensified two- or threefold. It's a no-win situation if you don't find the means to speak your mind to the director in a way that's both sensitive and diplomatic.

Most directors *want* your input; in fact, they need it for clarification. So, at your first meeting, *negotiate your relationship*. Simply put, find out *how* the director wants to work with you and, in turn, explain *how* you want to work with him/her. Spell it out in clear terms. Leave nothing unsaid. If you want to sit through every rehearsal and talk to the director after each session, say so. If you want to continue to rewrite all the way through opening night, say so. If you don't want to do any rewrites, say so. If you want to have some control in casting, say so. Say everything that's on your mind. Then have the director talk you through his/her process and how she/he envisions your participation. You both, then, can agree or disagree on how you're to function in rehearsal and talk it through until you're both happy. This may be simplistic, but I think in any director-playwright relationship, there should be a real sense of *we're* doing this together, *we're* going to make this work, *we're* going to solve problems and make this production successful.

When I've seen the relationship between playwright and director break down, it's because they stopped (or never started) communicating with each other or didn't decide how each would work with the other in the framework of the process. All of this can lead to confusion in rehearsal, disintegration of trust, back-and-forth blame tossing for something that's not working in the play, and a malaise or hysteria that affects the entire production team. The good news is that it never has to happen if you, the playwright, consider the following:

1.   A director's primary responsibility with your play is to illuminate your intention in the play and guide the actors, designers, and technicians through a process that will support that intention. But like actors, each director has a unique process

56

of creating. Don't panic on the first day or even in the first week of rehearsal if it feels to you like nothing is happening, but do ask about the director's strategy if you're concerned. Have her/him explain the process to you—you'll feel better.

2.   If, at your first few meetings with the director, she/he's talking about the play in various shades of "blue," and you see the play as completely "red," say something. Acknowledge your differences. Voice your concern. If the director insists on "blue," you've got a problem. These kind of problems usually don't get better, so depending on the situation, either you have to resolve your differences or someone has to walk away, and since it's your play . . .

3.   In this day and age, good directors are often great dramaturgs. They're trained to look at the full arc of the story, the details in the text, the structure of an act, the objectives of the central character, and so on. It is not uncommon for a director to suggest to a writer that a moment can be created dramatically without the words that are already written. They can also spot a moment that's overwritten or underwritten. How? They have these glorious things called actors that they're molding into the characters you've written, and they can see if an actor has trouble or not making an emotional connection. Listen to their advice. Talk about their suggestions. Always try to understand what's being said beyond the simple suggestion.

4.   Part of a director's job is to salve your wounds and calm your fears. Don't be afraid to tell your director what's going on emotionally for you as you watch rehearsal. That helps him/her better understand your vision of the play. On the other hand, don't worry the production to death. You have to have a certain innate trust that the director is going to deliver the play and production on time and that it will be something you'll both be proud of.

5.   Be prepared for a director to tell you that she/he doesn't want you at every rehearsal. This decision can be made for a variety

of reasons, but if it's made, ask why and get an answer. Sometimes directors just need the time alone to focus more intensely on the actors without you being involved. Oftentimes, they just need a break from your watchful eye. Maybe they want to try a cut in the text and don't want to alarm you until they're sure it works. Whatever the case, it's not a punishment, so don't treat it as one.

6.   As with anyone who works on your play, thank the director at the end of the process. And if for some reason you didn't see eye to eye, find a place somewhere in your heart and soul to gather the strength to be a better person, shake his/her hand and say "thanks." The theatre community is very, very small; you never know who knows who, so it behooves you to remain noble at times.

7.   Always remember the power of these words and use them: "Let's try it," and "Let me think about it." When you're in a rehearsal and something's not working the way you've seen it in your head a hundred times, approach the director, explain your thought, and empower yourself with the ability to say, "let's try it"—the worst thing that can happen is that you see what you suggested doesn't work. And if you're in rehearsal and the director approaches you with something that's not working in the script and wants to cut, alter, or rearrange the text, empower yourself with the ability to say, "let me think about it," and then do just that. Many a great line or monologue has been cut on impulse. Don't do it.

Designers

There is no greater thrill for me than sitting in the first production meeting of my play, watching the costume, scene, and lighting designers make their presentations. I feel like a kid, thinking, this is all for my play! because they've been thinking about the play, researching, ingesting the research, and making preliminary, then final, sketches and models. It's a rush—the same rush I feel when a good director talks about the play intelligently to the actors. In that moment of creative exchange, you can finally relax and say to yourself, "They got it. They understand it. The play is what I thought it was."

By virtue of their process, designers will come in and out of your production consciousness. You'll see them early on in rehearsal, then disappear for a while, then reappear later in the rehearsal process, closer into production. If you keep your eyes and ears open, you can learn volumes about your play from a designer because they're translators—they take what is evident in the script, combine it with their own imagination, and create the look of your play. They find and/or create all the nuances of your story and theatrically realize all of the dramatic possibilities within the world you've written.

Designers have three masters to please: themselves, the director, and you. This is tricky business and requires the true spirit of collaboration to be present. Your responsibility is to make clear in the text whatever's important to you by way of costuming, stage space (interiors and exteriors), lighting, set pieces, and special effects. If a red velvet couch in the living room of your central character is absolutely essential in your mind, you better write it in. If having the ability to see the interior of the living room and the exterior of the front porch is important to you, make sure it's in the text. If "Mom" always wears hosiery that's spotted with holes and tears, write it in.

A designer looks for clues—a direction—in the text and then creatively elaborates on those clues. If you're not specific in the text, you're allowing the designers to interpret freely. There's nothing wrong with that if you understand that what they will present to you will be solely their interpretation of what you've written.

Too often I see writers sit helplessly by during the design process. We fear we don't have the expertise or authority to say something, but *we are the authority* on that story that's being presented. Nobody knows that world better than we do. If you see something in the design concept that doesn't agree with your dramatic vision, say something. But be able to articulate why you don't think a design element is appropriate—that's helpful. Just not liking something because it doesn't appeal to your aesthetic is not helpful. You can guide the designers and the director into the world of your play by being specific in the text and even more specific in discussions in design meetings; that is the time to talk—not when you arrive at the theatre and see the set three-quarters constructed and the costumes on the backs of the actors.

Dramaturgs

The first question a lot of you will ask is What are they? They *have been* a lot of things: historian, researcher, developer, script doctor, visionary, and wordsmith. It seems, though, that coming into the new millennium, the role of the dramaturg is something akin to having a really intelligent, insightful, sensitive friend looking over your shoulder while you write, asking you all the right questions to sharpen and focus your play. Dramaturgs are still a relatively new position in the theatre—a position that most theatres in the country don't have the luxury to staff—but if you're fortunate to work with a skilled dramaturg, it could be one of the most rewarding experiences you'll have in the theatre.

A dramaturg's primary objective is to get to know the world of your play, to highlight for you those areas that need strengthening, and to illuminate for you those areas that need more clarity. Like any director, designer, or actor, every dramaturg has his/her own process. Often the process begins with a round of questions: why did you write the play? What are you trying to say in the play? What about the subject matter are you drawn to? What are you concerned about in the writing? A dramaturg's questions are not a challenge to your artistic integrity or the integrity of the play. They're designed to make you think about what you've written and to lead you into making your own discoveries about the strengths and weaknesses of your play.

Don't be surprised if your dramaturg's questions go from the very general to the very specific. She/he's on a mission to make your writing dramatically compelling, true to your intention and honest in its presentation. Don't be alarmed if she/he asks you to explain the climax of act 1, the metaphor of the yellow umbrellas in act 2, or the curtain line: "What? No more water?!" Simply asking you a question about the text doesn't imply that it's unclear. Perhaps the dramaturg's looking for affirmation of his/her own thoughts or ideas. When in doubt, ask.

Like any other relationship you have as a writer in the process of creating theatre, you should emotionally negotiate your relationship with your dramaturg. How do you want to work with this person? How can she/he be helpful to you? What does she/he need from you? Because chances are your dramaturg will be as unfamiliar to you as your director, it may take a few work sessions to build a trust between you that will serve your play. Since every dramaturg's process is different, ask yours to talk about the process and how she/he expects you to figure in. Talk to him/her. Share your own questions, doubts, revelations, and triumphs about the work. Be up front about your writing habit, or more specifically, your *rewriting* habit. Let your dramaturg know what your process is. This is a special relationship you don't want to waste. Use it. Challenge yourself and your play, but resist the temptation to defer your better judgment to someone simply because she/he can speak intelligently about your work.

Public Relations

Depending on the size of the theatre, the people who publicly promote your play can be anything from the director's best friend (who's a visual artist and works for free) to a whole department of people that strategize the best possible avenue for generating interest and gathering an audience for your play. All collaborative artists, at one point or another, have to allow other artists and administrators to do what they do best. Public relations people are no different. So while you have to allow a graphic designer to creatively conceptualize the idea for the poster, program, show logo, or flyer, you can offer suggestions and reactions to what's presented to you. If I have a choice, whatever represents my play in any kind of public print is something I want to be consulted about.

Too often, particularly in small theatres, the effort to get the play produced takes precedence, and details about promotion are decided apart from the playwright, who's then surprised when a flyer, program cover, or poster with a graphic has nothing to do with the theme of the play. I've been disappointed too many times when I've read a descriptive blurb that appears in my local newspaper and don't recognize the story of my play in the description. When it's appropriate, ask up front if you can read any print copy or review a graphic associated with the production of your play. And can we all agree to stop being "cute" in

61

program biographies? Is it just me, or is anybody else tired of reading, "David Thompson is the world's most brilliant playwright (and a great hockey player and french toast maker). Thanks to Mom, Dad, and my cat, Paws, who snuggles with me every night. Meow!" If you want to be taken seriously as a writer, present yourself seriously.

Audience

I'll often ask playwrights whose work I've listened to in a reading who the audience is they're writing for. I don't know why I'm always surprised by the blank look that meets my question. Playwrights sometimes adopt the idea that it doesn't matter who their audience is; they write for whoever will listen—an "it will find its audience" attitude. That's Bullshit with a capital B. Do you honestly want to leave your work up to that much chance? I contend that you have to know who you're writing for from the moment you sit down at your computer because it has a direct influence on every creative decision you make writing the play. Don't misunderstand me: the identification of your audience doesn't "write" your play, it informs it.

If I'm writing a play to tour high schools, and my mission as a writer is to educate my audience about the consequences of unsafe sex, I better understand—on some level—the mind of the teenager. I have to know their colloquial language, attitudes about sex, and principles about family and relationships, and I have to appreciate their wavering sense of self-awareness. To write a play that I want to be strictly commercial and play in every community theatre in the country would imply that I understand the basic complexion of the "community." What are their values, beliefs, religious convictions, and politics? If I know that the kind of theatre I'm writing is poetic drama, full of visual metaphor, dance, sound, and allegorical characters, wouldn't I be wise to ask myself what kind of audience appreciates that and where can I find them?

This is not to say that you shouldn't write a play that will challenge the politics or beliefs of the community theatre crowd, for instance. But you should know the fight you're up against. You should know that if you want to write mainstream, Broadway-type theatre, Broadway audiences are a very curious composite of humanity. Ask yourself, where do they come from? What's their attention span? What kind of day or early evening do they have before they get to the theatre? Do they want a simple escape from their lives or to be taken on a journey that will challenge their intellect and stimulate their imaginations? How far can I push the envelope with them? One thought to consider: you may not be concerned with who your audience is, but I guarantee any producer concerned about the future of his/her theatre is.

What a great feeling when an actor thinks your work is beautifully written or when a director loves your writing style or a designer thinks your play is full of richly woven metaphors and visual imagery. But what does it matter that we've created the most compelling piece of dramatic literature we're capable of writing for the theatre if it doesn't generate an appropriate response from the audience? Not only do we write for a specific audience, we write for the right reaction. We want an audience's laughter, their introspection or thoughtfulness. We want them to talk about the play at intermission and hope they'll leave the theatre still discussing the issues you posed in the play. We want some sort of tangible proof that the message we intend to deliver is, in fact, delivered.

Look around you—there are invaluable lessons to be learned from your audience once you get them into the theatre. Watch when they shift in their seats, read their programs, fan themselves, whisper to one another, wrap and unwrap their candy, or stop laughing in a comedy. If an audience gives you a consistent undesired reaction in performance, something's going on in the text that needs to be addressed. If you're smart about it, you'll make some notes, look at the play, and make your changes. Laughter is an obvious reaction—you can hear it, observe its duration, listen for its buildup or abrupt end. In a drama, the audience's reaction is obviously far more subtle. Watch your audience listening. Are they engaged? Are they restless? Are people looking at their watches more than at the stage?

An audience will give you the most immediate review of your writing. When they're bored, you'll know it. When they're engaged, you'll feel it. When they're confused, you'll sense it. Their collective reaction will point to a lull in the dramatic action, the success of a riveting, climactic scene, or the appreciation of wit in a monologue. Of course, none of this will happen if you don't open yourself up to watching their reaction.

So much to think about, huh? There are so many people involved in the production of one small play that it is never about one person's single vision, one idea or direction. It's a collaborative, creative process that requires you as the playwright to stay present, to actively involve yourself in decisions about your play, and to communicate your ideas well beyond what you've written on the page. You can't control everything and you know what? You shouldn't. But you should know enough about what every artist and administrator does to support your play to give you the most satisfying production. The theatre's a great playground to have fun in, so make friends and build your castles in the sand, together.

Who Needs an Agent!?

The first agent I ever solicited took the bait and asked me to submit a sample of my work. I dutifully and responsibly delivered my work right into his own hands. A week went by. Then another, and another. I called. He said, "Oh, right. I'm getting to your work this week. I'll call you." No call. Nothing but long, painful silence. Three more weeks go by. I call again. He says, "Oh, right. I'm sorry. Listen, something came up and I'm just getting to all of my reading this week. I'll call you." No call. Nothing. Painful silence again. Another two weeks go by and we both appear at the same party. I see him, he sees me, he walks directly to me and graciously, sincerely apologizes. He assures me he'll read the work over the weekend and call me on Monday. No call. Nothing. More painful silence. Two weeks later I get a letter in the mail with my play.

Dear Gary:

I've read your work, and I honestly have to say, it didn't grab me.

Jack

I wrote back:

Dear Jack:

Here's hoping one day I can *grab* you, and throw you down a flight of stairs.

Gary

Think I had something to learn?

Well, I learned it quickly. I moved to New York City in September 1986 and snagged an agent by January 1987. Didn't I think I was hot stuff? Yeah, I thought the sidewalk I walked on sizzled beneath my feet. I couldn't wait (was practically frothing at the mouth), to say out loud for the first time to a group of playwriting friends, "My *agent* is reading it now." And I signed with a big agency—one of the biggest agencies in the country, housed in an old, impressive granite building in midtown Manhattan. I couldn't wait to write on the front page of my manuscript: "Represented by . . ." Ohhhh, you couldn't tell me I wasn't headed for the big time. Then reality set it: I signed as a "nobody," stayed at that agency for four years as a "nobody," and left to go to another agency as a "nobody." What happened? Simple: I wasn't ready for an agent.

What good does an agent do you if you don't have anything to sell? And that's what an agent does—she/he sells your work and invests in the future potential of you as a significant artist. I had all the potential in the world, but when I signed with my first agent, I had little product, baby, and the product I did have was not commercial by any stretch of the imagination. So what was she/he going to sell? My good intentions? Yeah, it was great to know that I was signed. It was a terrific feeling; an absolute stamp of approval; the ultimate validation that I wasn't fooling myself, that I *did* have talent someone recognized. But an agent can't sell your raw *talent*, they have to sell what your talent creates.

There's no need here to invest in all the doomsday scenarios of the theatre (there's no money in the theatre for anybody, few people really make it, few theatres are producing original work, blah, blah, blah). But when an agent takes the action to sign you on as a client, they have to assume (in good faith) that you can and will have a career in the theatre because that translates into some sort of emotional or financial payback for the time they invest. You have to show extraordinary promise in a single play or the same in a body of work to initially attract the agent, *then*, deliver work beyond your signing that an agent can foresee has a future in the theatre. No matter how skillfully you write or how daring the theme or subject matter of any one given play is, if there isn't a theatre that can or will produce it, what's an agent to do with it? It's not to say there aren't exceptions to every rule, but on the whole, you have to imagine that if an agent is going to sign you, it's because there is something that indicates that she/he *should sign you* beyond the one lone play that drew their initial attention.

When I finally got smart about finding an agent appropriate to where I was in my career (two more agencies after my first agent), I had written a lot of plays—ten-minutes, one-acts, full-lengths—and was fortunate to have had a number of small productions at a variety of venues in New York and elsewhere. When I wrote my letter of inquiry to potential agents, I had a full production of a play running in New York. Potential agents could see the work on a stage or read it on the page. Also, I had a couple of theatres in the country interested in doing a production of one of my plays, and I had just finished a screenplay, so *I looked like I was busy—that I was hustling a career* instead of just waiting for someone to take care of me. It worked: I had five offers (three serious, two half-interested).

In this day and age, an agent has to justify your existence on their already overcrowded client list. Chances are, if you have few plays or productions to your name, it's going to be hard to secure an agent because the writer demand is way smaller than the theatre supply. An agent has to know, if not immediately, that eventually your work will find its way into several venues, not just one theatre; that there is an interest in your kind of writing and your subject matter; that there is something unique and different about you as a writer well beyond what's currently fashionable. They have a desire for you to work just as much as you have the desire to work so it behooves them to identify your potential.

Most of the agents I've worked with only did two or three things for me: negotiated a contract, submitted my plays in the "agent submission" categories of the *Dramatists Sourcebook* and the *Playwright's Companion* when I prompted them to, and helped me discover what theatres would be most receptive to my writing. That's my experience; I do know some writers who are fortunate to have an agent who initiates relationships between writer and theatre, and even more rare, who function as a dramaturg/literary advisor. You'd think these would be actions agents would take for their clients, wouldn't you? But the harsh truth is that agents are incredibly overworked and harried, and have ten, twenty, or thirty or more clients they're overseeing at any one time. They can't always give you the one-on-one attention you expect. You, then, have to do a lot of your own work until you reach a certain level in your career, or gain a solid reputation in a theatre that's just waiting for your next play.

Before running yourself ragged and feeling a swell of defeat after ten rejection letters (or no response at all) from writers' representatives, make an honest evaluation of where you are in your writing and your career and *why* you think you need an agent. If it's to promote the one good play you've written, to break into a theatre that's been ignoring your submissions, or to validate your existence as a playwright, it may be difficult to get an agent. If it's to cultivate a growing interest in your work by a number of theatres, directors, or literary managers, it may still be difficult. However, if it's to take you to the next level of your career after garnering a number of readings, small productions, playwriting awards, and contests and to nurture artistic relationships you've built in the theatre, then your chances of getting an agent are better. The bottom line is this: you'll secure an agent when you absolutely need an agent (when your play is being professionally produced), or when you demonstrate that there is good cause for you to be represented.

When you feel you're finally ready to seek representation, follow this very simple advice and I think your chances of being read and considered will increase:

1. Research the different agencies available to you. Not all agencies represent all kinds of writers. Know which agencies are more inclined to the Sam Shepard kind of work as opposed to those that have a fondness for more commercially constructed plays.

2. Write a letter of inquiry. Don't waste your time or money sending an agency your play if you're not sure the agency is in a position to accept new clients; (agencies are smart that way—they only have as many clients as they can reasonably promote). Include in that letter a brief biography, summary of your work to date and where it's received attention, and a very brief summary of the play you'd like to send them. All of this should be one page long—maximum—and should NOT be cute: "I want to introduce you to a playwright that will change your life and make you a million dollars!" Don't do it. And include a resume with your letter.

3. If you get a response back to your letter of inquiry, inviting you to submit work, don't send everything you've ever writ-

ten on the chance they'll find something they like in the pile. Send them what you consider your best work. They'll appreciate one solid play over three that are not fully developed. If you don't know what your best work is, ask a friend, teacher, or colleague.

4. Once you've sent your letter, DON'T CALL THEM. This is truly a "don't call us, we'll call you" enterprise. When they've read your play (and it could take months), they'll either write or call. Unfortunately, some agencies have been known to do neither. I know the temptation is there to follow up with a phone call, but if you do anything, write them a gentle reminder letter that they haven't responded to your submission. If you become known as a pest, you'll never get the positive attention you're looking for.

5. If you don't hear from an agency after you've submitted your work and written the reminder letter, take your anger and frustration out by any means other than direct confrontation with the agency. That'll get you nowhere quick. Besides, you'll rarely get to the person that was directly responsible for your play. Instead, you might find yourself heaping your anger on some poor, frazzled intern.

6. If you get a response letter from an agency saying they liked your writing but didn't connect to the particular play you sent them, write back and ask if you can send them something else that you have or something you'll have in the future.

7. It is not uncommon for an agent to suggest that they will represent the play you've submitted but not sign you as a client. What this means is—like it or not—they have to discern if there is interest in your play from theatres they have connections to, and if they get a positive response and, even better, have a theatre interested in producing it, they'll sign you. It's your call whether you're comfortable with this kind of relationship (sometimes phrased as a "freelance" relationship, or "hip-pocket"—as in, "I'll keep your work in my hip pocket").

The actual relationship with an agent is often complicated by the value you put on them and the power you give over to them. Boy, I've really had to learn the hard way on this, so learn from my experience. From the moment you sign with an agent, recognize you are in a relationship in which you both should be working on your career. I can't expect my agent to do all the work; conversely, I shouldn't be the only person promoting myself or my work. I can't expect my agent to have only me and my plays foremost on her mind, and to drop everything when I call or read my play the second it gets in her hands. Intellectually I've always understood this; emotionally it didn't make a difference how I intellectualized it. But even now I have to remind myself that agents are business people who have a lot to do, and while they don't want to appear like they're ignoring you, it often feels like they are. And I shouldn't expect my agent to love everything I write—if I do, I'm just setting myself up for heartache. Finally, I can't equate the physical time an agent spends on me to her level of interest in myself or my career—that's not an accurate gauge.

I know it's important for all of us to feel like there is someone who believes in our work enough to say, "sign on the dotted line." It feels good. It feels real. But like any relationship that we want to succeed and prosper, it has to be the right match at the right time. So while you're waiting for that to happen, write, self-produce, submit your work to theatres, take classes, join writers groups, apply for grants and fellowships, form relationships with directors and actors—make a creative life instead of waiting for it to be made for you. Do whatever you can to make yourself as attractive to an agent as you possibly can for where you are in your career. You'll be one step ahead of the game.

New York Hits Back

I hit New York thirteen years ago. It quickly hit back. Live in this city for a month and see if you don't get a good, old dose of reality slapping you right upside your head. Don't get me wrong: "New York, New York, it's a helluva town," alright . . . and hell on you. Expensive? Fuhgettaboutit. Dirty? Better than it used to be, but yeah, you don't want to trip in the street and put your face down on the pavement. Manic? Yeah, you need earplugs and horse blinders just to walk the street. It's a crazy place with a lot of crazy people attacking their lives instead of living them.

I wish I had a nickel for every time I heard someone say, "It's a great place, but I wouldn't want to live there." Here's the good news: as playwrights, you don't have to. That's right. *You don't have to live in New York City to be a playwright.* I don't know how that got started. Alright, I admit, it's the premiere theatre city in this country, if not the world. And granted, there are thousands of actors and directors crawling out of the woodwork. And yes, I can't deny there's a little off-off Broadway theatre in every neighborhood, but does that mean you have to live here to be a playwright? No. So let it go. That's why God invented mail and airplanes. Maybe it's not feasible, reasonable, practical, or convenient to live in New York right now. Maybe it never will be.

More people than you'd imagine buy into the idea that you can't be a serious writer unless you live in New York. Hello? Where did that come from? Should you visit? Yes. Live here? Not necessary. But if you do have some flexibility in your life, come. Move. Get here. Or make a decision to move to the next best thing. Let me tell you why: this is a theatre town—live theatre is everywhere and you need to experience as much of it as you can. You should see first-hand the novelty and profound enlightenment in the all-male version of *Romeo and Juliet*, the wit of the latest, slick British import, *Art*, the searing character portrayals in *The Beauty Queen of Leenane*, the lunacy of *Fool Moon*, the absurd good fun of *The Blue Man Groups' Tubes*, the acrobatics of De La Guarda's *Villa Villa*. Yeah, it takes money. But on any given day in any part of this town, there is free theatre or showcase theatre (there are hundreds a year) that'll cost you the price of a meal at McDonald's. You can be a kid, and the theatre in this city can be your candy store.

By seeing so many different kinds of theatre in whatever city you find yourself in, things happen: you learn from other writers; you see what the creative possibilities of the theatre can be; you meet important people in the theatre; you begin to associate certain theatres with the kind of work they do; you develop a critical eye; you discern fashion; you learn the names of the important people who might have a role in your career. It's a win-win thing. Sure, there are going to be bad experiences; you're going to see some real junk. But you can learn even more from that—what good directing should be, what an actor can and cannot do for the text, how a set and lighting design works for or against the play.

In New York and other big cities, theatre people are everywhere. You need for your own growth as an artist to get to know them. The cashier at my local Barnes and Noble performs in *Electra* at night. My next-door neighbor is a lighting designer at the Manhattan Theatre Club. The guy at the dry cleaner's who checks in my clothes is a playwright, too. My accountant is on the board of directors at Pulse Ensemble Theatre on Theatre Row. My doorman's niece is an intern in the literary department at Playwrights Horizons. If you're smart about it, you get to know them, they get to know you, next thing you know they're asking you if you have anything that's ready for a workshop or reading because everyone's looking for the next great play.

In New York, there's not just one playwriting class to choose from, there are thirty, forty, fifty of them. And they're good for what they are. There is not one small theatre that daringly does original work: there are a hundred small theatres willing to give you the break you're looking for. There are sit-down readings, staged readings, workshops, showcase productions, benefits, theme festivals, Broadway, off-Broadway and the like every day of every year.

Regardless of where you are, do something about your connection to the theatre. If you live close to Chicago, Seattle, Los Angeles, Dallas,

Philadelphia, Minneapolis, and so on, there's no excuse. Get in the car, make the trip. There's free theatre everywhere. Get to know some of these places you keep sending your work to. Learn who they are and what they're about. If you're not near a big city, plan a pilgrimage once a year. Immerse yourself in the theatre scene there. Call people. Look up who's who in the *Dramatists Sourcebook* and call them. Explain that you're a playwright and ask if you can come in and meet them, or ask if they offer a weekend workshop for playwrights, or if they can suggest a playwright's group in the area. In short, explore the resources you do have and don't minimize what's there because it's not New York. You don't have to be here, but you do have to understand and learn the world you're trying to play in and that world is around you.

A playwright friend of mine, Wendy, recently told me of a conversation she overheard in a playwright's group wherein some snob/jerk/loser playwright proudly said, "Oh, I never read plays. And I never, *never* go to the theatre. What for? Theatre people bore me." I asked Wendy his name. I'd never heard of him or anything that he'd written. Hmmmm.

Instruction or Destruction?

My first college experience was a big disaster. Not many people know this, but I enrolled in a college not far from my home town, took a full course load, and failed all six courses. That's right: all F's. Can you imagine? And one course—I swear—was a "How to Study" course. That should have told me something right there. What a nightmare. The reason for my failure was very simple: I wasn't ready to go to college. My head wasn't there. My heart really wasn't there. But I knew the thing I was expected to do when I graduated from high school was to go to college. So I went and I flunked out in a grand way. I wish I could tell you I learned a good life lesson then; I didn't, though. I was just a kid. Life lessons meant nothing to me at eighteen.

A year went by, and I enrolled at another college, desperate to find what I was going to do with my life. It took me a long time to figure it out, beginning with a bachelor's degree, then jumping into a master's, then sliding into a Ph.D. program. Through it all, I became no clearer about what I ultimately wanted to do, but I did discover one thing: I loved school. I loved the security, routine, systems in place, organization, bureaucracy, hysterical struggles with financial aid, sleepy all-nighters, all-day study sessions, endless rehearsals, pampered productions, last-minute term papers, inspiring instructors/hateful destructors, classes that motivated me and classes I slept through. Every moment was an experience to me, and I thrived before the sheer challenge of it. Give me a goal and I turn into the most driven man you've seen on two feet.

There are a lot of you out there trying to decide whether to go to college and study playwriting or some other theatre art. Admittedly, it's a big risk because you walk out with a degree that may be spiritually and artistically fulfilling but might not put you in the best placement for a well-paying job. Some of you are coming right out of high school; others of you are working now as bankers, lawyers, accountants, or in advertising and trying to decide if you should take the plunge and return to college; still others of you can't afford college but know you need some kind of instruction. Whatever your situation, the end result, if you decide to study, will cost you time, money, and energy—things most of us don't have a lot of. So you have to be a smart consumer, savvy businessperson, sensitive artist, and tenacious journalist while researching your options. If you're going to spend twenty grand on a college education or fifty bucks once a month for a weekend playwrights workshop, there are things you want to consider when you have a choice.

First and foremost: who's teaching? Don't be shy. Ask. Ask for resumes. Read their biographies in printed material. You want to know who's teaching you and what they've written *recently*. Does your instructor have to be a playwright to teach playwriting? I would think so. If I had a choice between someone who's out there every day, trying to grind it out and make a success of his/her writing career—as you will be doing—or someone who has a deep appreciation for the art but doesn't practice it, I know what my choice would be. It's not to say that there aren't some fine playwriting teachers who have never written a play, but I would never consider taking an acting class from someone who's never been an actor on stage if I had a choice.

You'll also want to find out how connected the faculty is to the world you're trying to become a part of. A teacher who is a working professional artist brings so much more to the classroom than one who isn't. When I walk into the classroom, I can offer my students my experiences with my agent, my relationships in the industry, the lessons I learned as a writer from the theatre that just produced my play, the process of the actor who helped me discover the weakness in my script, and so on. One of my greatest frustrations in my own educational experiences was the presence of some faculty members that were about as connected to contemporary theatre—what's happening today—as I'm connected to the United Nations. I'm convinced that in this day and age, an instructor's professional life has a direct influence on his/her effectiveness as a teacher.

Once you've looked over the faculty, look at the curriculum and ask questions about it. What's the idea or strategy behind the curriculum as it relates to training the writer? How is it structured to develop the writer from the novice to the experienced, or from the experienced to the even more experienced? What are the objectives of each class—the completion of a one-act, a full-length play, or several short plays? Are the classes constructed around a lecture/discussion, or are they oriented more toward a workshop? How many students are there in a class—a vital piece of information because the number of students in the class plus the actual time spent in class will dictate how often your play is read and discussed. What nonwriting courses are available to enhance the education of a writer? And is the program academically oriented—designed more to give you a theoretic exploration of dramatic literature—or oriented as a conservatory wherein you will produce a couple hundred pages a semester?

Okay, so you've asked about the faculty, you've looked over the curriculum, and now you want to know one final thing: what can they do for you in the life thereafter? In other words, once you've had the training, once you've written all that you can in the time you have, what can they do for you and your work? Does the department or faculty have relationships with agents or theatres? Does the department or faculty have alliances with writing colonies, producing organizations, literary managers, publishers? Does the department have an internship program? Can you actually work in a local theatre during your time in school, or can you be placed in a theatre once you've graduated? As an alumnus, can you continue to call on the resources of the department, such as the use of theatre space, mailing lists, or prop and costume loan? Is there a mentoring program in which you can be introduced to a professional playwright in the area who can guide you or, at the very least, offer you advice?

Production of your plays is an arguable point for making a decision about where you study. College and university programs have a lot of different needs to satisfy, and it seems to me that it is the rare program that can and will fully produce an original student play. Ask, though. And if they don't regularly produce original work, ask about the regularity or feasibility of workshop productions, staged readings, or scene work with actors. It's essential that there be a mechanism in place to hear your work read out loud by actors. Is there a forum for actors, directors, and writers to collaborate together on original work?

Finally, ask about money. What scholarships are available? How are those scholarships awarded? If you don't get a scholarship your first semester or year, can you be awarded one in the second semester or second year? Which scholarships are need-based and which are merit-based? What loans are available? Can you argue with the federal government for more money? Can you argue more money from the school? Are there work-study positions? Teaching assistantships? Graduate assistantships? Leave no financial stone unturned. It's no time to be proud. If you need money, ask for it. If you don't need money, consider yourself extraordinarily lucky.

These same questions and inquiries apply if you're just taking one playwriting workshop in a small theatre somewhere initiated by the artistic director or accepting membership into a playwriting group. You want to know who's teaching or moderating it, what his/her credentials are, and how she/he is connected to the local theatre scene. You'll want to know if there is an advanced class or lab that proceeds the one you're interested in, if there is a forum to hear your work read, and if there is any kind of financial aid available or bartering system or deal you can work out to pay your way.

One last thing to do: visit the college, university, writers group, or playwrights lab before you make any kind of commitment and TALK TO THE PEOPLE THAT ARE LIVING THROUGH IT! Don't just talk to one person, talk to five, six, ten, twenty, if you can. Just think about it—any administrator worth his/her weight in salt is going to give you the slick, glossy version of their program. They want you to come. They want you to deposit your money in their bank. So get the down-and-dirty reality from the students that are there. I'd be highly suspect of any school or program that doesn't make current students available for you to talk to. And don't just talk to the students an administrator picks for you to talk to. Find someone in the hall, pull him/her aside and ask questions, or ask the administrator for the phone numbers of a few alumni willing to talk to prospective students.

Now the hard part: wherever you decide to educate and refine yourself, be it in college, a workshop, or a writers group, if it's not working for you, *get out.* I know these are sharp, harsh words, but why spend time in something that can be not only counterproductive but even destructive if it's not working for you? We fool ourselves into thinking that bad things get better over time. But with your time, energy, and money hanging in the balance, how long can you afford to wait before you finally accept that something's not working for you in the way you need it to work?

An unprepared teacher or negative group facilitator doesn't get better over time; a disorganized, unfocused group of writers doesn't miraculously focus itself; rampant destructive criticism doesn't get kinder over time. If you're writing absurdist comedy and the obvious fashion in the workshop is kitchen realism, the tide isn't going to suddenly turn for you. I'm not suggesting you jump at the first sign of trouble. Talk it out. Ask questions. Attempt to make it better for yourself. But if things don't change, get out of there. A refrigerator that doesn't cool is a refrigerator that doesn't cool, no matter how you plug it in. Why would you react any differently to a class or writers group that isn't working?

I took a playwrights workshop several years ago that was ill-fitting from the beginning, and I could kick myself even today for the four weeks I wasted waiting for it to be anything other than what it was. The workshop inevitably started late and ended late. The facilitator talked about himself *ad nauseam*, dropping names between every other breath and filling precious time with mindless details about his own career. The playwrights in the room were so defensive about their work that you couldn't suggest a comma placement in their text. They also served as actors and lacked any emotional depth in a reading. How useful was that? Most everybody in the workshop was bitchy—jaded theatre folks who tried to one-up each other with horror stories about their careers. It was a real party, alright.

Why did I hang on so long? Stupid Reason Number 1: No one else seemed to have a problem with it. Stupid Reason Number 2: What would it look like if I just left? What would people think of me? Stupid Reason Number 3: I paid for it and didn't think I could get my money back (of course, I didn't ask). Stupid Reason Number 4: I told all my friends I was taking this workshop and they were thrilled for me. What would I tell them now? Final Stupid Reason: It was better than nothing.

To learn and practice the art you love to create in an environment that you're excited about is a thrill like none other. It's all out there to experience. Finding it is sometimes difficult, but not impossible. And if you're wise about where you choose to enrich your mind and nurture your talent, you'll be given a gift for life—the security of knowing you've done your best to be the very best you can be.

Submitting Your Plays: The Most Necessary Evil

If you're Tony Kushner, Terrence McNally, August Wilson, or Wendy Wasserstein, announcing to the world that you've completed a new play must be like announcing to your family and friends that you're pregnant. The shrills of good cheer must be deafening. And with good reason. You've proven you've got damn good genes, you've been heralded, even awarded, for your previous offspring, and everybody wants to have a baby just like your last nine.

Anytime I write a new play, I timidly let it slip out somewhere between "pass the salt" and "it's good split pea soup, don't ya' think?" Fortunately, my good friends know me too well and gently ask, "So what's it about?" After I've spit and sputtered over my soup, repositioned myself in my chair for the eighth time, tried to change the subject unsuccessfully by posing a question about the Middle East, or offered up multiple uses for styrofoam pellets, I usually arrive at a dignified answer.

Okay, I admit it. I hate that question: *What's your play about?* I guess because every insecurity that I have about the play instantly rises to the surface, and I feel like I have to make the answer to the question as interesting as my play. Why? Because I'm going to get an instant review from my answer. The person asking the question will either say, "Oh, that's interesting," or "how funny" or "that's a great idea," or—my worst fear—they'll react like I had just explained the biomechanics of fig breeding: their eyes will glaze over, their faces will go blank, and I won't even get so much as a "hmmmmmmmm."

It's a challenge to answer that question—What's it about?—and yet now more than ever playwrights must be able to answer that question directly, concisely, and with enough compelling language to make even the most overworked and burdened literary manager respond to your letter of inquiry and synopsis with a, "Yes, we'd like to read your play."

The art—and I do mean *art*—of submitting our plays to soliciting theatres has become key, if not pivotal, to all of our writing careers unless we want to continue in that "showcase-as-meaningful-venue" syndrome. Frankly, I don't think I can sit through one more showcase of anybody's work, particularly my own. Not that I'm not grateful for any production of my plays. But I have truly been there, done that— worn the paint on my hands for days from touching up the set on opening night. And I'm thankful, but now I want something more. I want the *big* production at a theatre with real seats bolted into the floor! And I've discovered I can have it—if I know how to ask for it.

Whether you're submitting your play to a friend of a friend who is the cousin of the assistant literary manager at the Mark Taper, or you're mailing it out to a small theatre in Ohio that you suspect won't be in business by the time your submission arrives, submitting your play to theatres for their consideration is a necessary evil.

Let me tell you how much I hate submitting my plays to a theatre for their consideration: I'd almost rather walk a mile on a broken leg before I did it. It takes everything I've got to get it together to shoot one small script out to some small theatre in the mail. And if I'm skillful in finding ways to avoid writing a play, I'm brilliant when it comes to creating avoidance for sending it out. So let's just collectively get it out of our systems now:

YES! WE HATE IT!
NOBODY WANTS TO DO IT! (We'd rather be discovered)
IT TAKES TIME!
THE RESULTS CAN BE REALLY FRUSTRATING!
IT'S EXPENSIVE!
THEY PROBABLY WON'T READ THE DAMN PLAY ANY-
WAY!
WE HAVE TO BE ORGANIZED!
WE HAVE TO . . . (gulp) SELL OURSELVES AND OUR PLAY.

What other choice do you have? Look, I want to increase my odds of getting a production anywhere and everywhere. So if that means I have to sit my butt down for an afternoon, stuff envelopes, xerox my resume, bind my manuscript, and stand in a long, long line at the post office, so be it.

I resigned myself to this shortly after a production of my full-length play *When a Diva Dreams* here in New York. After months of rewriting, then seeing it up, still tinkering with it during production, and doing a final rewrite after it closed, I was convinced that the play was finally in good enough shape to send it out. What I didn't realize is that there is a whole system, an entire code of "playwright behavior" that has to be in place in order to effectively submit your play and then graciously wait for a response.

My first reality check came with the awareness that there are several fundamental truths about submitting your work that you cannot bend, reshape, reconceive or distort:

1. There are too many of us (playwrights) and too few of them (theatres who routinely produce new original work). Your first task, then, is to make your work known in such a way as to invite not only the submission of your current play, but any other work you might have. This starts with taking the time to *research* where and how to submit your play and then BELIEVING and honoring your research.

If you read the *Dramatists Guild Sourcebook*, the TCG *Dramatists Sourcebook* (the best listing I know of soliciting theatres), or the *Playwright's Companion* and the description of the submission process notes that the theatre is not looking for kitchen realism, BELIEVE IT. If the description says that you should submit from January to May, BE-LIEVE IT. If the description says that it'll take six months for a response, BELIEVE IT (then add two to four additional months). If the description says "agent submission only," BELIEVE IT. If the description requests ten pages of dialogue, don't send fifteen. If it says that the company is looking for plays with six characters or under, why would you send a play with nine? Do you think they won't see the other three? Or do you think that they'll be so taken with your play that the three additional characters won't matter? BELIEVE IT! THEY WANT SIX OR UNDER! Every artistic director and literary manager that I've had the pleasure of doing business with remarks consistently that writers either don't read, don't believe, or don't honor their submission descriptions.

2. Submit what the theatre asks for, nothing more, nothing less, *and make it easy for them*. Remember, you're trying to sell them something on their time. What's included in a submission package is a letter of introduction and inquiry followed by either a synopsis, and/or pages of dialogue, or the full text. This means you have to learn to write a business letter of introduction that (a) isn't cute, (b) isn't rambling, (c) isn't bitter, and (d) isn't so long that they might as well have read the play, but is (e) short and direct, acknowledging their particular interests and why your play is suitable for their consideration.

This introductory letter is their first exposure to your writing. Don't blow it off because it's only a letter. If it's just a letter of inquiry, include a self-addressed stamped postcard (SASP) that says, "yes, we'd like to read your play," or "no, we're not interested in this project." Then, all someone has to do is check it off and mail it back.

3. You have to learn to write a synopsis of your play. I know, I know. We all collectively hate that. But if you do your research, you'll see that more and more theatres do not want you to send your play—they want a synopsis. And they want a *good* synopsis that tells them the idea of the play, the style or genre, a brief description of the characters, and a description of the central conflict.

Things to avoid: "This is an uproarious comedy . . . " Let someone else be the judge. A five-page synopsis equals one minute of attention before it's tossed. Keep it short, probably a page. Don't be so clinical as to induce stasis. Use every creative writing skill you've ever been taught, and seduce the reader into wanting to see more. If you have any questions about your synopsis, give it to somebody who knows your play and ask for a fair assessment. You didn't write your play without feedback, why chance the synopsis?

4. Pages of dialogue should be able to stand alone dramatically and must represent the effort of the play. If a theatre requests pages of dialogue instead of the full text, what they are asking for is an opportunity for you to demand they read more. So what should you send? The opening? The climax? The end of act 1? This is your call, but what I'd suggest is that scene that made you weep for hours or laugh until you cried

while you were writing it. However, make sure that the scene can be understood out of the context of the full play. If there are too many inner-textual references to events or relationships in the play that the reader has no knowledge of, the chance for confusion (and disinterest) intensifies.

5. A full-text submission should be secured in a binder (*not clipped*), with page numbers visibly printed, a cover page with your name, address, and phone number followed by a character breakdown on a separate page and the text that follows. On the inside back jacket of the binder, staple your self-addressed-stamped envelope (SASE)—interns and literary managers will thank you.

Even after you've given the theatre exactly what they asked for, and your play is perfectly suitable for their theatre, and you've done your professional best to present the work in the most attractive way, there is one unavoidable reality: you might not hear back from them. Ever. Or it'll be months and months before you hear from them. Discouraging? Absolutely. But it's very real. Who knows what happens? After I had done my research for *When a Diva Dreams*, and narrowed down the theatres I thought would be interested in (1) an ensemble comedy with (2) seven women that addresses issues of (3) family and race and is set in (4) one location, I submitted everything from a simple letter of inquiry to a synopsis to pages of dialogue to over ninety theatres across the country. Of the ninety, this was the result:

Number of theaters saying "yes, we'd like to read the work": 32
Number of theatres saying "no, we're not interested": 28
Number of theatres I never heard from: 30

Of the thirty-two who said "yes, we'd like to read the work," ten followed up with "we read the work and it's not for us," (I wrote a thank-you-anyway letter). Eleven followed up with "we read the work, we liked it a lot, but we're not doing it," (I immediately wrote a thank-you letter and of course asked them if they'd be interested in reading another play of mine). Five said "we'd like to hold on to it for further consideration" (I'm still waiting, but I haven't called; I won't call; you shouldn't call; *Don't Call! Trust me, they'll call you when and if they're in-terested*). Four are still reading it (two years later—you know what that means), and three committed to a production (they'll get my firstborn).

With the thirty I never heard from, I wrote a second letter express-ing my continued interest in their theatre with a gentle reminder of my submission. I eventually heard back from twelve of the original thirty; eighteen are still missing in action, and though I'm tempted to list every one of those theatres by name, I'm well aware that so many small-to medium-sized theatres are truly dying out daily or struggling just to stay alive.

Submitting your work to a theatre is business. We're talking time, money, energy, effort, patience, perseverance, and so much that has so little to do with writing a play. But now I know how. Is it worth it? You bet—I enjoyed those three productions. Are there shortcuts? Please, let me know. Can't my agent do this? He is—we're both doing it. He does the "agent submissions only"; I do the rest. The way I see it, the more eggs in the bowl, the better the soufflé. Is it hard to stay positive? Of course. Can you beat the odds? Of course. Would you give up if you got no response? No way. I'm a writer. I've got something to say. And I want to share it with as many people as I can.

What You Need Is a Good F**k

I've often heard people say this—to other people, of course. I actually overheard this yesterday in a local bar/restaurant. My eyes darted about to discover the source: two Wall Street, Brooks Brothers types sipping beers and drawing circles in the spilled table salt with their fingers. I discreetly looked up from my five-alarm chili and tried not to be an obvious ear in their conversation. After they traded playful insults and manly jabs, Wall Streeter Number 1 tells Wall Streeter Number 2 that he's noticed his performance is slipping, that he's lost his edge, that he used to be (I'm not joking here) a "Tiger with Big Teeth," but now he's gone limp. He's got no fight. Wall Streeter Number 2 hangs his head and quietly admits, "I don't know what my problem is," to which Wall Streeter Number 2 offers, "You need a good f**k, man, that's all," then gives him a quick slap on the back.

I don't know that I agree with Number 1's testosterone-informed assessment of Number 2's problem, but I do know what the man-as-animal was doing. A friend knows what another friend needs because of the way that person *behaves*. Our behavior doesn't lie. It gives us away. It brazenly displays our emotional life without so much as a "Mother May I?" And if we're writing about people in the theatre, wouldn't it stand to reason that we know what our characters *need* as a way of creating their behavior?

Playwrights often measure their success by the amount of free-flowing creative ideas that are ready-present to write. And if that moment comes (and it always does), where there are no great ideas for a new play right at the front of our consciousness, we fret and question our talent and title as "play-wrights." Fellow writers and students of mine often approach me with that self-tortured, I-don't-have-an-idea-I-don't-know-what-to-write look on their faces. My first response to them is, "What do you need?" The look on their face is replaced with an I-need-an-idea-for-a-play-you-idiot—that's-what-I-need look. But what

I'm telling them is to dig deep down inside themselves, connect with a personal need they have as a human being who's lived on the face of this planet for any length of time, and start there as a basis for generating character and story. Frankly, I think it's this simple:

NEEDS = BEHAVIOR = POTENTIAL CONFLICT

I don't think this is revolutionary, or necessarily even original, and by no means anything new to actors, who look for what their character needs when they work through a role. But as writers we sometimes overlook the obvious in our haste to be creatively complex.

If I need to be the center of attention (and blush, blush, I often do), and you need to be the center of attention, and we're at the same birthday party for a common friend, there's the potential for conflict—conflict between you and me because we want the same thing and by definition only one of us can have it; conflict with the rest of the folks at the party who are pinned against a wall as you and I roll on the floor tearing each other's hair out; conflict from the Birthday Girl who's pissed that we've taken the spotlight off her and put it onto us.

NEEDS = BEHAVIOR = POTENTIAL CONFLICT

It's fail-proof. If I'm driven by an emotional need, I undoubtedly behave a certain way, depending on the circumstance, that could increase the dramatic tension around me and put me in conflict. And the intensity of the conflict is directly related to how bad I want what I need. If I have a desperate need for companionship, and you have a proportionately desperate need to be left alone, instant conflict. If I have an intense need for adventure, and you have a softer, gentler need for a more quiet way of life, instant conflict. If I'm a lawyer that has a dominating need for justice and I've been hired to expose your company for wrongdoing and you, out of loyalty to your company, need to demonstrate that loyalty by hiding the truth, instant conflict. What could be simpler?

If you're looking for an idea for a play, start with a need—say, independence and autonomy, put the need on some made-up character—say, a mother and housewife—put the housewife in a circumstance that forces her to express or repress that need—say an overbearing, socially uptight husband, then sit back and watch the conflict build (Ibsen wrote his version of this in *A Doll's House*).

People need all kinds of things. Consider these few examples:

Achievement	Acquisition	Adventure	Affiliation
Balance	Change	Conformity	Companionship
Creativity	Destruction	Dominance	Endurance
Enjoyment	Loyalty	Power	Reverence
Romance	Sex	Sympathy	Success

You can take any one of these and begin building a character, a scene between characters, or a whole play based on one person's simple need in conflict with another person's identical or opposing need. Of course, no one person is any one thing. We're motivated by any number of things. But start with one need, then add another, then another, and see what you get. Go on. Try it. See what happens. Or would you rather sit in front of a blank page for hours trying to think something up to write? Give it a shot!

Back to the bar: when I heard Wall Streeter Number 1 say, "What you need is a good f**k," I was tempted to walk over and say, "What you really need is a friend that can look beyond the superficial to see if there's something really troubling your soul." But I *need* to keep my face intact, and they were way bigger than I was. So my need to be everybody's counselor was quickly tempered by my need to finish my chili and keep my world in balance . . . at least for the moment.

T-Minus-Ten and Counting

First there was the full-length play about a gajillion years ago. Then some sassy playwright got daring (or maybe bored, or low on ink) and thought, "Why do in three acts what you can do in one?" So the one-act play became the *genre du jour* until God created television and MTV. Then some clever writer thought, "Why do in one-act what you can do in ten minutes or in a monologue play?" Shortly thereafter, God created Jane Martin and/or the Actors Theatre of Louisville, and the great submission flood rivaled its biblical equivalent. But sadly, pretty much every playwright's ten-minute play drowned in the flood.

So God created the *Dramatists Sourcebook* and the *Playwright's Companion*, and lo and behold, there appeared the One-Page Play. Wonder if God's going to create an audience for it? (If so, expect the next Great Flood). Pretty soon we'll have the No-Page Play—just a lot of playwrights lined up at the door of a literary manager, who sits patiently listening to a writer say, "Just imagine a play . . . and it's really funny . . ." I personally am going to lobby for a new genre: The Three-Day Play— a sort of Tony Kushner-meets-Eugene O'Neill-weds-Disney-divorces-the-Nederlanders kind of thing.

Call me reactionary, but I get scared when I see my art form shrinking with such enthusiasm. Don't get me wrong, I like the Ten-Minute Play. In fact, I love it. I should. I've written enough of them. I love them so much I started a Ten-Minute Play Festival at NYU and another for the Kennedy Center's American College Theatre Festival. So I'm a big fan . . . with big reservations about how and why we write them, and even bigger cautions for when we produce them.

My first and biggest concern about the ten-minute play is that we're creating a new genre for a generation of writers who aren't necessarily proficient or prolific in the long forms. Personally, I'm hesitant (but do it anyway) to teach my students to learn the ten-minute play form when I know they haven't fully embraced the one-act play, let alone the full-length play. And I think I'm frightened with good reason: this is a generation of students who were raised on television. They know the world in sound bites and outtakes. Their television programming, commercials, and films are doled out to them in fifteen- to thirty-second images that flash only the condensation of emotion, with little screen time spent watching those emotions develop. They are used to an abbreviated expression of creativity that I have to constantly work against. When I teach them the ten-minute play form, am I only reinforcing what potentially ails them in the first place?

No, not if I make a commitment to teach and *expect* them to use the same skills and creative know-how in writing the shorter form as with the long. And maybe that's where all of this goes awry. Shouldn't the ten-minute play be exactly that? A play with a beginning, middle, and end, with compelling characters, rising action, and resolution that lasts for ten minutes? It shouldn't be what amounts to a scene or a sketch; it's probably not a monologue; definitely not a dance/poetry reading/choral ode to the universe's ecosystem.

What it should be, then, is a self-contained story that advances a conflict which pushes dramatic tension to some sort of resolution and (gulp, I hate to use this word) catharsis, no? Does that mean it has to be naturalism, kitchen realism? No, I wouldn't think so. It doesn't mean that in the long form, so why would it have to be so in the short? But it does mean that there is little to no time to engage our audience; the temptation to be clever or cute, and write "idea plays" that are thin on ideas could become overwhelming.

My second concern: with a new genre that is constrained by an actual time factor (or number of pages) comes the challenge of trying to convince everyone to learn the *art* or true skill of writing within its limitations and not try to defy or bend the definition of the form. As I said, I've produced a festival of ten-minute plays for the last five years at NYU and for the last three years for the Kennedy Center. Let me tell you some of the ways writers try to scam the system:

1. Changing the font on their typeface so a writer can cram fourteen pages into ten. Hello? Is it me, or is this as obvious as the British invasion on Broadway?

2. Expanding the margins from the usual one-inch parameter toward the edges of the page to fit more script in. Is it me, or is this as obvious as the Disney logo in Times Square?

3. Shrinking the spacing between character names, dialogue, and stage directions to fit more script in. Is it me, or is this as obvious as another year of *Cats* on Broadway, despite the video for PBS?

4. Writing beyond the ten-minute (ten-page) limit to eleven, twelve, thirteen, fourteen pages "because surely you're not talking to me" or "the brilliance to be found on page twelve is worth the exception." Is it me, or is this ego as big as an Andrew Lloyd Weber bank account?

Look, I'm for anything that gets writers writing and theatres exposed to more voices. But a ten-minute play will go where? Most likely in a ten-minute play festival for the Theatre Behind the Bowling Alley because (1) they're relatively easy to produce, (2) audiences are treated to a diversity of voices, (3) they're great opportunities for actors, (4) they're a terrific challenge for designers, and (5) theatres are introduced to a number of new playwrights they can nurture and cultivate relationships with. So if you're going to write in this genre, be smart about it:

1. Consider not setting your play in the kitchen of a four-star restaurant that requires three ovens, two stoves, five waiters, and two dueling chefs preparing an eight-course dinner for the President. Remember, somebody's actually got to produce this! And they're counting bucks, people power, favors they're owed, connections they have, and the hours in the day to produce not just your play, but six or seven others.

2. Consider cutting your Dancing Sailor Chorus from fifteen to three. If you do that, you've got those three, the Captain, the Captain's boyfriend, the Captain's boyfriend's boyfriend, his lover, his lover's father, and his lover's father's parrot (I know it can be the stage manager dressed in green garbage bags and a smart yellow cap, but he still has to be counted). OK, that's a total of nine people in ten pages. Wheeeewwwwww! That's a lot of folks in a little time. And can you really get an actor

to do the part of the Captain when all he does is limp on stage with an oak branch as a cane, look at the Dancing Sailor Chorus, and say, "Velveetta, anyone?" It's not impossible, but I think it'd be a hard sell.

3. Consider cutting at least twenty of your thirty sound cues, and the same for your fifty-two light cues, unless you want to see a very haggard and intensely cranky tech crew. Not to mention that in ten minutes, your play could look and sound more like a video clip from the People's Choice Awards on television.

4. Ten minutes means ten minutes, so consider having a reading of your play before you send it anywhere. Wouldn't it be a drag to get a call from an artistic director who says they'd love to do your play if you'll considering cutting five minutes out of it? In the longer form, that's the equivalent of cutting act 1 from a three-act play.

If you're new at producing ten-minute plays, consider the following; if you're a writer, learn to appreciate what has to happen just to bring your ten-minute play to production:

1. You're producing eight shows no matter how you slice it. So you need a support staff that can accommodate those numbers—whatever that means to you. At NYU, it means eight directors, one set designer, one lighting designer, one costumer designer, one production stage manager, and a crackerjack running crew. The running crews have to change sets, set props, re-patch the dimmers and cue the CD player or tape deck multiplied by eight in one evening just for preshow, let alone what happens in the interior of the play.

2. You *need* a production stage manager beyond the individual stage manager for any one play (if you can afford to have that luxury). Why? Traffic. Lots of it. Loads o' people—everywhere; too many people who need to be in too many places at different times. *Someone* has to coordinate everybody's effort. You need a person in charge that's not trapped for hours at any one play's rehearsal—someone at home base who can see and understand the *big* picture and organize it.

3. The scene and lighting designer will have murder on their minds if you don't allow them to design the evening of work with a unit set and rep light plot. Trying to accommodate eight locations for eight very different plays interpreted through the eyes of different directors becomes a logistical nightmare. Of course, the challenge is to represent the individuality of each play into the working whole, but that becomes the designer's challenge and a welcomed one, I might add, over the alternative.

4. Do eight plays mean eight directors? Your call. Economics, people resources, and their time are certainly a consideration. It's eight additional people to deal with, but maybe you have eight directors whom your company needs to serve.

5. Remember, eight (or six or whatever) plays translate into eight different rehearsal schedules, eight different tech times, eight different casts, and eight different playwrights to consider. Think of it like a big, complicated musical—a kind of *Sunset Boulevard* meets the Radio City Music Hall Rockettes has an affair with Edward Albee and you'll begin to appreciate what it takes to get *that* goat up on its feet.

6. Programs and publicity: Names and biographies for days. Postcards that look like a page out of your local phone book if you try to cite everyone involved. The volume of biographies in the program can approach mythic proportion. Just anticipate it and you won't be caught off guard.

Ten-minute plays are fun, a challenge to write, and interesting and enjoyable to experience when they're done well. But let's go forward into the new millennium with a clear head about it: shorter doesn't mean easier on any level. Ah, there's the rub. Ten-minute plays are harder to write and produce than any of us think, but maybe we haven't spent much time thinking about them because it's all so new.

Do We Have to Say This?

Yeah, maybe we do, because a lot of playwrights still don't get it when they submit their play to a theatre or simply give it to someone to read. OK. For the record:

1. *Number the Pages of Your Manuscript.* A couple of excuses I don't buy: "My computer does it automatically and I haven't figured it out." Figure it out. "I'm waiting to do all the rewrites to do the final pagination." Don't wait. Do it now. If I drop your play on the floor, and the pages scatter in different directions, the last thing I want to do is figure out how it all fits together. Give me a break. Number your pages.

2. *Secure Your Manuscript in a Binder.* Blue, red, yellow—who cares? Just make sure that the pages of your manuscript are *bound—brought together by some measured force*—in a presentation folder or three-hole punched with brass brads. Three-ring binders take up a lot of room on anybody's desk or file cabinet. I wouldn't use them. Staples come unstapled. Paper clips fly off into oblivion. You can't lose with a presentation folder that has silver, metal clasps that bend back or with the brass brads.

3. *Put Your Name, Phone Number, and Address on the Title Page.* Make it easy on me. If I've read your play, and I want to share my ideas with you, I don't want to spend time searching for your phone number, even if you think I have it. If I'm a theatre considering production of your play, it's a courtesy to me that you make it easy to contact you.

4. *Identify the Sex and Age of Your Characters on a Page Directly Proceeding the Title Page.* Necessary? Absolutely. As a producer, I want a quick reference for how many characters are in your play and the ratio of male to female. The name *Terry* could be a man or woman. Let me know which it is.

5. *If You're Submitting Your Play to a Theatre, Weigh It Before You Mail It, and Put the Appropriate Postage on It.* Come on! You've gone through all that work to write the play, and now you're taking the time to submit it to a theatre. Go the extra distance. Care that it gets there and back to you with the proper postage and in one piece. A SASE or SASP should be stapled with the appropriate postage affixed to the envelope on the inside back jacket cover of your presentation folder. That way it doesn't slip out or get lost or mutilated in the shuffle.

6. *Title Your Play!* Surely you've lived with it long enough to find an appropriate title. It's important. It's the first thing I read and the first image created in my mind of your work. If you insist on *Untitled*, then I insist on creating a blank image in my mind, and you're responsible for working harder to fill in the picture. There's no magic formula for writing a title, but a surefire solution is to look for an active verb in combination with some noun: *Driving Miss Daisy*, *Waiting for Godot*, *Dancing at Lughnasa*.

Consider these six small courtesies to the person who reads your play. They may seem trivial, but to the literary manager or producer (who reads hundreds of plays a year) they are not. These people will immediately notice and appreciate your attention to and care of all aspects of your craft, and they will think kindly on you as they read your play.

* * *

JUST . . . FOR GOOD MEASURE

(Maybe you know this stuff; maybe you don't.)

* * *

Just Read It, Will You?

A play reading is like a blind date—when it's good, you can't believe you're so lucky and you want to praise every form of God there is; when it's bad, you're just waiting for it to be over, hoping you won't be scarred for life and that you can walk away from the experience without vomiting on someone's foot. And like a blind date, there's always a huge bout of trepidation until the big moment arrives and you quickly learn how the evening's going to play out. I don't know about you, but I never liked blind dates. Hated them, as a matter of fact. On the other hand, I've learned to like, even love, the mystery and adventure of a play reading because I finally figured out why readings exist for the playwright, what I should expect from a reading, and what I need to do as the writer to be absolutely prepared as best I can for the eventuality of it all.

I can't imagine a play being considered "finished" until there's been at least one reading, if not two or three, somewhere in its development. If the live theatre process includes *spoken* words that drive dramatic action and an audience's reaction to the placement, rhythm, and structure of those spoken words, isn't a reading absolutely necessary to any creative development? We cannot remove the theatre audience from the process of creation—they contribute too greatly to the whole event. There is no better venue for a writer to integrate an audience into the process of writing the play than a reading.

As painful as they can be sometimes, I'm as excited about the reading of a new play of mine as I am about its first production, because readings are my molding clay and I'm an eager sculptor. I can shape, re-shape, or cut away whole scenes; redefine characters and strengthen the plot line before and after I've heard a reading of my play. I can tweak and torque my words to within an inch of their syntax, watch my audience's reaction, and figure out all I need to know to move the play forward in its development. I can watch actors stumble over lines and simplify the dialogue. I can watch a director struggle with my long monologues and dense scenes, try to quicken the pace of the action, but lose the battle because of my writing. I can confirm that a dramatic moment works brilliantly, just as I envisioned it, or watch it fall flatter than a pancake, just as I feared.

Play readings are my tryout, a test for my doubts and a confirmation of my intuition. They are my selfish tool—meant only for me, the writer, to hear the strengths and weaknesses of the play and to clarify the text based on the audience's reaction. By virtue of their abbreviated rehearsal process and truncated production values, they are *not* meant to showcase the talents of my director or actors—they will be rewarded much later, in actual production. It is a *playwright's* forum, and if I take care of my end of the business before an audience hears the first word, I can focus on why I have a reading in the first place—to hear the text.

The first question I ask myself prior to a reading is, Do I need a director? More times that not, I confirm that question with a "yes." If I have a choice, I want someone other than myself who likes and understands my work to bring the presentation of the text up to a level that an audience can appreciate so that I can stay focused on the writing. Once I've found a director, we should decide together what the objective of the reading is and plan the presentation based on that understanding. If I want simply to hear the text and nothing more, perhaps a minimally rehearsed, sit-down reading will suit the work best. If I want to hear the text and get a sense of the physical, dramatic action, perhaps my director will incorporate modified blocking with actors holding their scripts. If I'm fortunate to have the script worked on in a developmental workshop where I can watch every rehearsal and rewrite the script, and I need a stronger sense of the actor's craft to bring the full life of the play to the surface, perhaps my director will plan a more formalized, completely staged reading with sound and minimal props. Whatever we decide to do in rehearsal and performance, it's important for everyone involved—especially the actors—to know what our common goal is and how the creative team (the director and myself) expects to achieve it.

Play readings must be an extraordinary challenge for actors in that there are so many limitations imposed on them in this very tightly controlled presentation. They can't move about or fully use their bodies to convey any sense of character or build a dramatic moment. They have to spontaneously interpret words on a page and make sense of them, and have no external trappings (sets, props, costumes) to help form a more complete image of any given dramatic moment. Consequently, it is the responsibility of the creative team to make the actors' work as headache- and hassle-free as possible.

The second question I need to ask myself is, Do the actors know where I am in the development of the play, what we hope to achieve with the reading, and how we want the actors to contribute to the process? Actors need to know what's expected of them to gain and maintain a solid base for their work: if it's to be two casual table readings of the play wherein actors bring questions to me about the text that need clarification or explanation, the actors should understand that. If the director and I want more of a polished performance with actors more off-book than on, and I want to make significant changes to the text during the rehearsal process on the spot and expect the actors to integrate those changes instantly, the actors should be warned.

Once everyone's clear about what exactly will go down in the rehearsal and performance, I should do anything I'm capable of as the playwright to assist the actors' ease in translating my words from the page to the stage. To start, I should talk about my characters in as much detail as time will allow. The actors need a jumping-off point to think about who their characters are, why they take the actions they do in the play, and what their significance is to each of the other characters in the play. In a short rehearsal period, they need all the dramaturgical help I can give them and will appreciate my input. I should let them ask me as many questions as they have and try to fill in the gaps in their character understanding.

I should also give them a script that is easy to spot-read (not necessarily double-spaced; perhaps a space and a half), particularly if I have long, dense monologues without any character interchange. I should remember that they have to read my text live, and if they stumble to keep track of where they are physically on the page, I lose any sense of rhythm, cadence, and flow of dialogue. Don't underestimate this. If you have a script that looks like this:

DAVID

Why aren't you coming with me? I spent all day yesterday, and the day before, and the day before explaining to you in detail why it is important that you come to this company picnic with me. Jesus, Beverly, I know you don't like Mr. Gruder. I know you hate these social things. I hate them too! But I have to go! And I have to bring my wife. Everyone brings their wives. And everyone hates it! And they all hate Mr. Gruder, but we have to pretend we like him or there won't be any Christmas bonuses. And I need that Christmas bonus. WE need that Christmas bonus. If you want to have a baby, and I think you do, we can't do it without the Christmas bonus. The bonus is key, baby. It's key to our happiness.

I guarantee an actor will stumble all over the dialogue unless they have the text memorized (and how likely is that for a reading?). Also (and I know this is not a very popular idea among writers), I should punctuate my dialogue. Punctuation is to dialogue what quarter notes, half notes, and whole notes are to music. They instruct the interpreter *how* to read the words. I'm often amazed that a playwright is surprised that an actor didn't make sense of a passage of dialogue when it's punctuated like this:

DAVID

Well okay if that's what you really feel. I mean you have a right to say what you feel don't you. And I respect that Beverly, I really do. And just so I'm clear for the record I don't really want to go either but I have to go because my job depends on it and if that doesn't matter to you what am I going to say?

Sure, an actor can eventually figure out the sense of the lines, but there isn't much time in a reading to waste, so why shouldn't I help the actor out?

DAVID

Well, okay, if that's what you really feel. I mean, you have a right to say what you feel, don't you? And I respect that, Beverly, I really do. And just so I'm clear for the record, I don't really want to go either. But I have to go because my job depends on it. And if that doesn't matter to you, what am I going to say?

Also, I should pronounce any odd words, colloquial phrases, or cultural indicators that my actors have no reference for, and I should explain any quirky behavior I see clearly in my head as central to a character.

I can do everyone a favor by not acting in my own play, no matter how strong the temptation and how perfect I am for a character I've created. If I act in my own play, I'm an actor concentrating on my acting, and not a writer concentrating on my writing. My concentration simply can't be in two places at one time, and for the betterment of my play, I need to be a writer. Most important, I should make sure my actors (and I know this sounds obvious), *actually understand the play I've written* and not just the lone character they're creating. They need a sense of the dramatic arc of the play, and a short rehearsal period doesn't always allow for that kind of understanding.

My director has his/her own responsibilities to the reading. She/He should work to ensure that each actor understands his/her character's emotional life in the play, and to solidify relationships between characters. She/He should question me about anything that feels underwritten, overwritten, metaphor heavy, dense, or elliptic. She/He should encourage or, if she/he has to, impose a pace on the reading that will keep it alive during performance. She/He should question me about what staged directions are absolutely necessary to be read for the audience's comprehension of the action (nothing bogs down a reading like endless stage directions read out loud) and make sure the actors understand what written staged directions will be read for the audience's comprehension of the action. And finally, she/he should either read the staged directions her/himself, or find a competent actor to do it. On this, I've learned my lesson the hard way: a reader who slogs lifelessly through the staged directions can bring the reading to a veritable halt.

I can't hear another bad reading of a play that I've written. I can't do it. I refuse to do it. It's too painful, too disappointing. I've worked too hard on actually writing the play to see it slaughtered in a public reading because I was careless about my responsibilities or the director's and actors' responsibilities in the creative process. So I'll be active in the rehearsal process, do everything I know to do to ensure its success, and not sit passively by like another piece of furniture in the rehearsal room, watching my play being created around me. I care too much.

Just Show Me How to Do It

Alright, enough with the words of encouragement and spiritual support! You need some hard and fast stuff to at least get you in the right ballpark to play your game. There is no ideal model for this, and everyone does it differently, but I've tried to gather enough information from a variety of sources to present you with a clear idea for an effective letter of inquiry, a playwriting resume, the standard format for the text of your play, and the order and look of the first three pages of your manuscript.

The Submission Letter or Letter of Inquiry

GENERAL TIPS: Keep it short. Keep it way short. Don't try to be cute. Don't try to be clever. Don't try to grab your readers' attention—they've opened the envelope to read your letter; that's attention enough. Give them the facts and sign off. Let their energy go toward reading and responding to your play, not your letter. And make sure in the letter you list everything they've asked for in the solicitation, then make yourself a checklist and include everything they've asked for (Figure 1).

The Playwright's Resume

GENERAL TIPS: First question—what do you do if you don't have a lot of readings or productions to put on your resume? Whatever you do, DON'T LIE! Don't say you've had a reading or a production of a play at a theatre that you haven't had. You'll be found out and look worse than someone who has a thin resume. If your resume is thin, list the plays that you've written, a brief synopsis of each of the plays, cite any classes or workshops you've taken as a playwright, and detail any other experience you have in the theatre (such as stage manager, director, actress, dramaturg, etc.). People are more likely to be sympathetic to you being young in the theatre than they are to you being someone who misrepresents yourself.

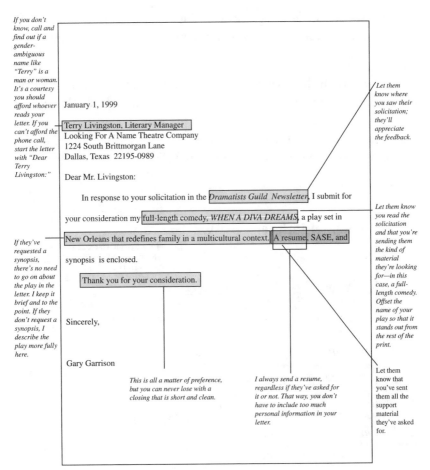

If you don't know, call and find out if a gender-ambiguous name like "Terry" is a man or woman. It's a courtesy you should afford whoever reads your letter. If you can't afford the phone call, start the letter with "Dear Terry Livingston:"

January 1, 1999

Terry Livingston, Literary Manager
Looking For A Name Theatre Company
1224 South Brittmorgan Lane
Dallas, Texas 22195-0989

Dear Mr. Livingston:

In response to your solicitation in the *Dramatists Guild Newsletter*, I submit for

your consideration my full-length comedy, *WHEN A DIVA DREAMS*, a play set in

New Orleans that redefines family in a multicultural context. A resume, SASE, and

synopsis is enclosed.

Thank you for your consideration.

Sincerely,

Gary Garrison

Let them know where you saw their solicitation; they'll appreciate the feedback.

Let them know you read the solicitation and that you're sending them the kind of material they're looking for—in this case, a full-length comedy. Offset the name of your play so that it stands out from the rest of the print.

If they've requested a synopsis, there's no need to go on about the play in the letter. I keep it brief and to the point. If they don't request a synopsis, I describe the play more fully here.

This is all a matter of preference, but you can never lose with a closing that is short and clean.

I always send a resume, regardless if they've asked for it or not. That way, you don't have to include too much personal information in your letter.

Let them know that you've sent them all the support material they've asked for.

Figure 1. Sample Submission Letter

A more accomplished playwright's resume should list the productions or readings of plays (including the theatre and the date), awards, grants, writers colonies you've attended, workshops you've participated in, festivals your plays have been invited to, and any special recognition you've received as a writer. I try to give the reader a sense of my whole writing career, so I include my membership in theatre groups, professional organizations, and related writing work. This may sound obvious, but if you don't include your address and phone number at the top or bottom, you've made a big mistake. Put it on the resume and cover sheet of your play and obviously on the return envelope (Figure 2).

Script Format

Everyone's got his/her own idea of how a script should appear physically on the page. Remember one simple fact: your writing has to be read, so make it easy for the reader. The example I give you is pretty standard with the exception of the internal stage directions, which are often off-set in the center of the page and italicized (Figure 3).

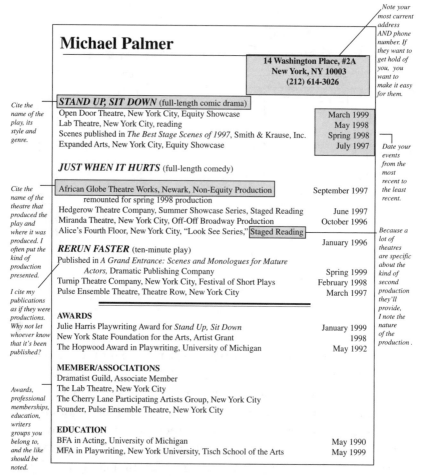

Figure 2. Sample Production Resume

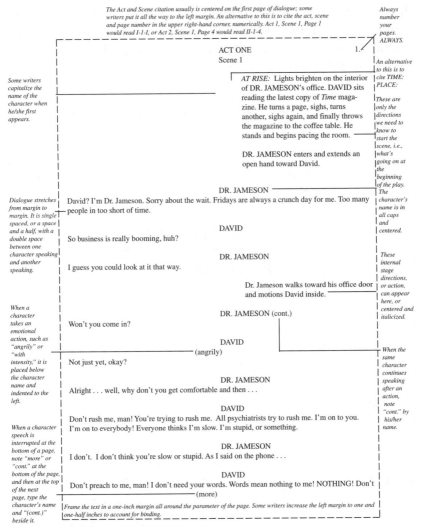

The Act and Scene citation usually is centered on the first page of dialogue; some writers put it all the way to the left margin. An alternative to this is to cite the act, scene and page number in the upper right-hand corner, numerically. Act 1, Scene 1, Page 1 would read I-1-I, or Act 2, Scene 1, Page 4 would read II-1-4.

Always number your pages. ALWAYS.

ACT ONE   1.

Scene 1

An alternative to this is to cite TIME: PLACE:

AT RISE: Lights brighten on the interior of DR. JAMESON's office. DAVID sits reading the latest copy of *Time* magazine. He turns a page, sighs, turns another, sighs again, and finally throws the magazine to the coffee table. He stands and begins pacing the room.

These are only the directions we need to know to start the scene, i.e., what's going on at the beginning of the play.

DR. JAMESON enters and extends an open hand toward David.

Some writers capitalize the name of the character when he/she first appears.

DR. JAMESON

The character's name is in all caps and centered.

David? I'm Dr. Jameson. Sorry about the wait. Fridays are always a crunch day for me. Too many people in too short of time.

Dialogue stretches from margin to margin. It is single spaced, or a space and a half, with a double space between one character speaking and another speaking.

DAVID

So business is really booming, huh?

DR. JAMESON

I guess you could look at it that way.

Dr. Jameson walks toward his office door and motions David inside.

These internal stage directions, or action, can appear here, or centered and italicized.

DR. JAMESON (cont.)

Won't you come in?

When a character takes an emotional action, such as "angrily" or "with intensity," it is placed below the character name and indented to the left.

DAVID
(angrily)

Not just yet, okay?

When the same character continues speaking after an action, note "cont." by his/her name.

DR. JAMESON

Alright . . . well, why don't you get comfortable and then . . .

DAVID

Don't rush me, man! You're trying to rush me. All psychiatrists try to rush me. I'm on to you. I'm on to everybody! Everyone thinks I'm slow. I'm stupid, or something.

When a character speech is interrupted at the bottom of a page, note "more" or "cont." at the bottom of the page, and then at the top of the next page, type the character's name and "(cont.)" beside it.

DR. JAMESON

I don't. I don't think you're slow or stupid. As I said on the phone . . .

DAVID

Don't preach to me, man! I don't need your words. Words mean nothing to me! NOTHING! Don't
(more)

Frame the text in a one-inch margin all around the parameter of the page. Some writers increase the left margin to one and one-half inches to account for binding.

Figure 3. Sample Format Page

The First Three Pages

A potential producer or literary manager needs a quick reference at the beginning of the manuscript to make an intelligent decision whether they're capable of producing your play. The first page of your manuscript should be a title page, the second page should be a character break-down, and the third should be an act-by-act, scene-by-scene listing. This form should be incorporated from the shortest ten-minute play to the longest full-length play (Figures 4–6).

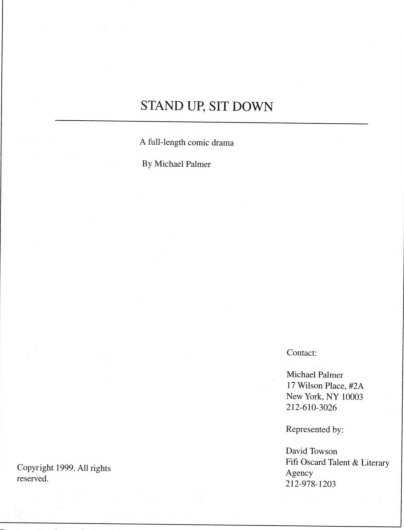

Figure 4. Sample Title Page

Characters

WENDY TULIPS, F. 41	Former actress, educated, well-read, loves to eat pork, has a secret.
NOONIE TULIPS, M. 40	Wendy's husband. European, kindhearted, talented writer, just on the verge of success.
ROCCO TULIPS, M. 18	Wendy and Noonie's son. Loves all kinds of music. Hates sports.
VANESSA MARCY SINCLAIR, F. 32	Mysterious. No one knows her real name. Novelist, eccentric, gregarious, beautiful. Cleans a mean bathtub.
LESLIE GEE-CAN-SHESINGO, F. 39	Opera Diva. Beautiful, talented, dark, Italian.
MAGGIE MANKEM, F. 38	Teacher, spiritualist; raised in Long Island. Always troubled by her hair.
MUSTACHE SALLY/THE PAINTER/THE COOK	Actor #1
RADIO CITY LISA/THE ACTIVIST/WOMAN #1	Actor #2
AUNT LINDA/WRITING PARTNER/ CAKE DECORATOR	Actor #3

Figure 5. Sample Character Page

SETTING

The interior and exterior of the Tulips' Upper West Side apartment in New York City.

TIME

1999 and ten years prior.

ACT ONE

Scene 1: The interior of the Tulips' apartment, dawn, 1999.

Scene 2: Four days later, evening.

Scene 3: On the stoop, outside of the Tulips' apartment, night, 1989

ACT TWO

Scene 1: Rocco's bedroom, dawn, 1989

Scene 2: On the stoop, outside of the Tulips' apartment, night, 1999

Figure 6. Sample Scene Breakdown Page

Just Give Me the Facts

I almost cringe at the title because there are very few facts in this business. But what follows is a list of questions I'm always asked when a group of playwrights assemble, so let me try to knock out some answers that have some (?) demonstrated and historical reality to their answers.

What Do I Do with My Play Now That I've Finished It?

That's always a frightening moment, isn't it? Here's this—embryo— that you've spent months, even years, developing, nurturing, coddling, feeding, and nursing along, and now it's finally born. You can hold it in your hands. It's real, it's tangible; it exists. You can finally see the fruits of your labor. Your first goal should be to confirm with intelligent readers (friends, directors, actors, and the like) that you have, in fact, what you think you have. Put your play before every set of eyes you trust and ask for criticism and feedback, but make sure you control the criticism that comes back to you. I've seen many a play ruined, or a writer totally paralyzed by feedback from a committee.

As you know, I'm a big advocate of readings, so I suggest that after you've heard the initial response from your intelligent readers and made changes to the text based on their response, the next step is to have several developmental readings of your play. If actors aren't readily available to you, don't sweat. Use who you know (your readers, for example; at least they know the play). Don't worry at this stage about what a real actor can bring to the experience—you just want to hear your play read out loud. Listen to your play like a fine piece of music; listen to the language, the transitions, the build in dramatic sequences, and the placement of character revelations. Remember, you can learn more about your play in a casual reading than you ever can by reading it yourself and imagining it in your own head.

Once you've finished hearing, reading, and making the necessary adjustments to your play, your next objective is to get it produced in a

109

modest venue or produce it yourself in a safe, comfortable atmosphere. A production—regardless of who does it—will strengthen the writing by pointing up the strengths and weaknesses (more changes?—you bet!) in the play that you then can correct either during or after the production. After all, what you really want is the tightest, most deftly written play you can create. Anything that brings you closer to that goal is worth pursuing. If it's only a well-planned, well-rehearsed black box production of your play with minimum production values, the feedback you'll get from watching that production (and the audience) will be all you need to take the play forward. It doesn't have to be at the Guthrie for you to learn something about your writing and your play. On the contrary, learn what you need to learn in a smaller venue, then send it to the Guthrie. A modest production might also attract agents, producers, literary managers, and if you're really lucky, an invitation for future productions of that play or your next work.

If, after your readings and modest production, you're absolutely sure the play is ready to be read by an often unforgiving stranger (intern, literary manager, agent, producer, director), submit it to as many institutions and working professionals as time and money will allow. The key to success here is your ability to research the resources available to you, discern where your play should be submitted most appropriately, submit the work in a professional manner, and then show up to the first rehearsal ready to begin your real work as a playwright.

There are two excellent resources for submission listings: the Theatre Communication Group's (TCG) *Dramatists Sourcebook* and the *Playwrights Companion*. Every theatre, agent, producer, writers colony, contest, festival, publisher, or writers workshop soliciting new plays and working with new playwrights in the United States is in one or the other of these books (and available at your local retail bookstore). Decide what your play needs in the next stage of development—a rehearsed workshop reading, another production, a workshop in a writers colony, money for future development, and so on, and find what opportunities cited in these two books can best satisfy your need.

The books are divided by category of opportunity, and list everything you need to know to make a successful submission. *Pay attention to the submission requirements, and send the institution* what *they ask for*, how they ask for it, and when they ask for it. The listings in either of these books will give you the name of the theatre, producer or agency, the artistic personnel involved at the theatre, the address, phone number, fax and e-mail address, their own particular submission procedure ("no unsolicited scripts; agent submission only," "prefers synopsis, sample scenes and letter of inquiry," for example), types of material they're looking for ("full-length plays or musicals"), the best times to submit your play, the response time, special programs and interests the theatre has, the physical facilities of the theatre and, oftentimes, production considerations ("unit set, no more than seven characters; running time no longer than ninety minutes"). If you have any questions about this, look back on the essay, "Submitting Your Plays: The Most Necessary Evil" on page 80.

A number of submission opportunities are also listed in the newsletter of the Dramatists Guild, (the international service organization for playwrights), along with feature articles by noted playwrights and dramaturgs. For your modest membership fee, you'll receive the newsletter and quarterly publication, the *Dramatists*, and you can call the Guild office for advice on performance contracts, attend invited lectures and seminars hosted by professionals in the industry all across the country, make use of the Guild's rehearsal room located in their offices right off Times Square, and most important, be connected to fellow playwrights throughout the world just by becoming a member of this prestigious organization. You'll need the services of the Guild once you score your first big contract, so get to know them beforehand.

How Long Is a Play?
A Ten-Minute Play: 10 pages; no more, no less
A Short Play: up to 30 pages
A One-Act Play: 30–50 pages
A Full-Length Play: 70 pages or more with at least two acts
A Foolish Mistake: over 120 pages

How Do I Get Published?
Have a production that's reviewed well. A publisher has to have something to publicize if you don't have an established name. The larger or more important the theatre that's produced your play, the better the

chances of its publication. If you have plays that can be associated with festivals or special interest groups (Actors Theatre of Louisville's Ten-Minute Play Festival, The Women's Project, Young Playwrights, Inc., Gay Plays, Theater for a Mature Audience, etc.), you'll stand an even better chance of publication.

How Do I Get an Agent?

You don't. They "get" you. But if you want to push the envelope (and why wouldn't you?), see page 65, "Who Needs An Agent!?"

How Do I Get Reviewed?

If you're in a metropolitan city, no one knows better than you how difficult it can be to get someone in to review your work if your play is being produced by a small, obscure theatre group. Of course, they'll never get there if they don't know that you're actually producing something, so spread the word . . . as often as you can. A press release followed by a personal letter to the Arts and Leisure Editor of your local newspaper, followed by another strategic press release followed by a phone call may almost be too much, but worth the chance. You'll want to pique their imagination in your press release ("world-premiere . . . gripping story of the Civil War . . . eight men . . . ensemble cast . . . based on the true stories of decorated Civil War heros."), make clear the dates, times, location, *and* request a reviewer. That's right. Don't assume just because you send them a press release they'll assume you want to be reviewed. Tell them in plain English.

If you're lucky enough to get a reviewer to your production, make it easy for them to find the theatre if it's not in a known location (send directions), make it easy to secure their tickets, find their seats (the best in the house), and at the end of the performance, personally thank them for making the effort. A word of warning: be careful what you wish for. Make sure the play is really ready to be reviewed before you make the effort to secure a reviewer. I've seen writers stop writing after a bad review, and I've seen reviewers stop responding to writers after a bad production.

Should I Ever Sign a First Right of Refusal?

This phrase, "first right of refusal," might come up in a conversation or negotiation you have with a director of your play. What they're asking for is the right to have the "first" option to direct your play should any-one want to produce the play at a different theatre. The Dramatists Guild and the Society for Stage Directors and Choreographers (SSDC) are at loggerheads over this issue. Until the big guys battle it out, I'd ad-vise you of one thing: it's difficult enough for a playwright to get his or her work produced at any theatre in this country; you can conceivably limit the appeal of a theatre producing your play if it comes with any kind of conditions. Ultimately, it's your choice, but understand what you're doing when you sign your play over to anybody. If pressed, offer to put your director's name forward to any theatre interested in your project whenever it's appropriate.

Should I Give a Producing Theatre Conditional Rights to My Play?

This will often be asked of you if a theatre is producing your play and wants you to sign a contract stating that the theatre holds the produc-tion rights to the play for six months or a year. What they're asking you—in the simplest way of thinking—is for you to grant them the right to produce your play *exclusively* for a certain amount of time. This is your call, but anything that takes my work out of the mainstream for a period of time makes me nervous. Theatres that produce the first pro-duction of your play will often ask that they be cited in print for that distinction. Nothing wrong with that. And they deserve it.

What If a Director or Actor Wants to Make a Change in My Script That I Really Don't Agree With?

First, really try to listen to what's being asked of you. After your de-fenses have died down, and you're sure your ego isn't the only thing re-sponding, make the decision that best serves your play as you see it and stand by it. You're the playwright. You have the right and option to say no. But also realize you have the option to change your mind.

What If I'm at Odds with an Actor or Director on How They're Approaching My Play?

If you're concerned about an actor, talk to the director and express your doubt or worry. A director can help you through understanding an actor's process and can conceivably calm your fears. If your problem is with the director, talk first to the director. Explain what you're concerned about. Give your director a chance to respond to your concerns. If the problem continues to exist, talk to the person (if there is such a person) who hired or secured the director. Again, voice your concerns with diplomacy and sensitivity. If the problem continues to exist even still, your options begin to narrow. I never like to be in a position where I feel I have to exercise whatever power I have, but if exercising that power means the difference between a good production and a bad one, I'll do it as kindly as possible.

What If I Want to Be a Screenwriter?

Baby, that's a whole different world and a whole different book. What I know (and what I have experienced firsthand) is that playwrights make great screenwriters because we inherently understand all the fine elements of solid dramatic writing: interesting, quirky characters; sharp, witty dialogue; and a compelling story. But the structure and writing style of screenwriting is a whole other kettle of fish. There is a proliferation of workshops and seminars being sponsored throughout the country, as well as several fine educational institutions, to get you started in this very difficult career if you're interested in pursuing it.

Just ... Think on It

"Just Do It!"—I hate that ad for Nike tennis shoes. Want to burn it every time I see it. And you can't miss it: black background, inescapable white letters. It's in every magazine I read, and though it's referring to sports, it might as well say, "Gary, we're talking to you, man." My first reaction is always defensive. I mean, how can you *just* do anything? God, if it were that simple, wouldn't I *just* be a Broadway playwright by now? And yet I shouldn't toss the *J* word away as some insignificant modifier that's got nothing better to do than to hang around a lot of action. There's something powerful about the word, *just*. Something simple yet quick, impulsive, demanding, and uncompromising. It's a do-it-now kind of word that begs for your attention. Just listen! Just look! Just think! It got me to thinking. So just . . . read on.

JUST that simple: My first directing/would-be playwriting teacher, a man who in his stocking feet was five-foot-one and easily weighed three-hundred pounds, pulled me aside one day halfway through the semester and growled, "Garrison, how many times have I told you, just because someone invented the word *just* doesn't mean you just have to put it in just about every line of dialogue. What's it going to take for you to understand that?" He then lit a cigarette, coughed a lung up, gave me a manly pat on the shoulder, and waddled out of sight. When the coast was clear, I whipped out my script that we read in class. Sure enough, on page one, I used the word *just*—no joke—eleven times. I won't even tell you how many times that word appeared in a twenty-page scene. What the hell was I thinking? Thinking wasn't the problem—I hadn't been listening.

I've only half listened to any playwriting teacher I've ever had—partly because I had a short attention span, but mostly because I was arrogant about my art. I would reason, "How could anyone but me *really* understand the flow, rhythm, or cadence of my dialogue or the arc, intention, or theme of my scene?" And when you listen to criticism of your work with that frame of mind, you can hear only half of what's said to you (if that much). Believe me, I always heard what I wanted to hear, but had selective hearing for everything I didn't want to hear. Now having taught playwriting myself, I wish someone would have grabbed me and throttled the arrogance right out of me. How many years of bad writing could have been avoided if I thought more of the person who was teaching me than I did of myself?

Ego is one thing, and it certainly has its healthy place in the psyche of all artists. But arrogance is quite another and, for a playwright, deadly to the craft of writing. The bottom line is this: if a climactic scene is boring, it's boring—it doesn't matter that at the end of the scene your central character's got a monologue that will make your audience convulse with sorrow. If your dialogue is stiff, it doesn't matter how authentic it is to the Blue Ridge mountain range. If a character appears directionless and unmotivated, it doesn't matter that she's going to single-handedly convert the world to Catholicism at the end of the first act. If it doesn't work, it doesn't work. Now in all fairness, if one person's critical comment doesn't resonate in you as a writer, OK. But if two, three, or four people all say the same thing, then do you want to be a good writer or do you want to continue to defend your choices to people you think don't get it? It's . . . *just* that simple.

JUST *read: Aaaahhhh*, the joys of living in New York. I'm having dinner with some old friends who bring as their guests a couple of really nice guys—one's a theatre director and his companion is in the movie business—or so I thought I heard. Actually, he's in the *moving* business, but I didn't realize that until way after I tried to present myself as a writer-in-the-know by asking him if he knew Blah-Blah-Blah at New Line Cinema, or Blee-Blee-Blee at Tribeca Film Center. His blank stare should have tipped me off, but I thought he was being Soho-aloof. While slathering a wad of babaganush on a piece of pita bread, the director said, "No, he's in the *moving* business. He *moves* people," at which point the mover says to me, "What do you do?"

A long beat. I offer, "I'm a playwright." Quickly, he says, "Yeah? I move you guys all the time. Moved a famous one yesterday." He turns

116

to his companion. "What was his name?" "Tony Kushner," the director says through a mouthful of potato chips. I try to remain casual. "Did he have lots of stuff?" I ask. The mover arches his back and stretches his arms high into the air, like he's just come off the job, and reveals, "You've never seen so many books in your life!" I immediately think of the three books near my bed: *Eight Weeks to Optimum Health*, *Windows 95 for Dummies* and *So You Want to Be a Jewish Mother?*—don't ask.

The mover pulls me out of my moment of self-loathing with, "Yeah, every famous playwright I've ever moved reads tons of books, mountains of books." Then he looks at me like he's got the big answer and says, "You wantta be famous?" I lean in to hear him say, "Take it from the big guys. Read. Books. And tons of 'em. And then, hey. It won't be long till I'll be moving you uptown." From his truck to God's ears.

The fact is I read plays all the time. But books? Who's got time? Well, I think I better make more time to read because the mover was right. Reading novels, essays, histories, biographies, fiction, poetry, even science and medical journals, stretches the imagination, broadens the intellect, nurtures the soul, and raises the spirit of creativity. It fills the well of the creative subconscious that we drain every time we write. If anything, literature in any of its glorious forms allows us to look at how someone else manipulates language to convey an idea, attitude, vision, or dream. And being that language is the primary tool of our trade, and the ability to manipulate it can make the difference between a play that's produced or not produced . . .

JUST a good idea: the Writer's Guild of America (the union for screenwriters and television writers) offers its members entrance to any film screening for *free* during different times in the year just by showing their membership card. I want that! I want that perk for working as hard as I do as a playwright who hasn't made it yet but needs a simple act of support. In New York, I want to walk into an Equity showcase of an original work and show some sort of membership card and not have to pay for a ticket (the same privilege afforded Equity actors if there is a seat available). I want producers of off-Broadway and Broadway shows to understand that the next great play that will appear on Broadway might be coming from me, and that it only makes sense to provide half-price tickets for me as a playwright so that I can see as much theatre as I can that will educate and inspire me.

JUST a request: let's strike from the vocabulary of people who teach playwriting or respond to new plays the words, "only write what you know." I've heard playwriting teachers, dramaturgs, respondents to readings, and scores of fellow playwrights say this to burgeoning writers and to each other with great alacrity. I have a sneaking suspicion everyone's forgotten what it really means and are only repeating what someone told them years ago. Personally, I don't buy it. If I only wrote *what I knew*, would I ever know anything else? I've always thought that I'm a much more interesting writer when I write about things *I don't know* and have to discover, research, and submerge myself in a world that is frighteningly unfamiliar.

JUST some nerve: Wait a minute, wait a minute! Let me see if I've got this right. I spend six months to a year refining, rewriting, and working on my play. All the while I'm working at Pizza Hut and the post office to pay rent and eat. Then I save and save to be able to afford postage to send my play to your theatre, and pay for the postage for you to send it back. Add in the cost of xeroxing, a binder, an envelope, and stationary to write a "read my play" letter—we're up to about ten, twelve dollars right there. Now . . . you honestly want me to PAY YOU to read my play?! You call it a "processing and reading fee" and I call it "easy money for you." And you're taking it from people who are notoriously poor in the theatre.

I know it's hard to find readers. Do you pay them with my fee? Or does that money go somewhere else? Why not apply for a grant and offer a workshop by a local dramaturg, artistic director, or playwright to teach a script analysis seminar and EDUCATE people on how to read a play. Use that group, then, as your first tier of readers. Or find a college theatre department or a local theatre group and ask for volunteers there to read the first tier of submissions.

Or do you ask for a fee to deter some folks from submitting, thereby limiting the amount of submissions to your theatre (I've heard on several occasions that this happens in some of our more reputable theatres). Who might you be turning away? Are you really willing to take that gamble? What if I'm brilliant and poor—like so many of history's greatest artists?

JUST remember: This is a small, small world. Ohhhhhhh, it's tiny. And you never know what a person's path is going to be. That dramaturg you snubbed (because you don't really understand what the hell a dramaturg is anyway) is tomorrow's literary manager at the Manhattan Theatre Club. That literary manager you badgered on the phone at Theatre in the Pine Trees is moving to the Mark Taper next week. That director you alienated because you kept talking to the actors behind her back during rehearsal will be opening the first show at the Guthrie next season.

JUST took a break from writing this, took a walk and saw this on a T-shirt: You're never given a wish that you're not also given the power to make come true.

JUST bite the bullet: I worship actors like a heathen. I have immense respect for their talent. I stand in awe at their perseverance, tenacity, courage, creativity, and their energetic support and kindness to writers. But, if there's an actor who's not working as a character in your play, let them go. Do it kindly, and as early as possible, but let them go. Too often I have stood by and watched something that I've written sink because either I myself, the director, or the producer made a bad casting choice. Yes, it's painful. But you're doing yourself and the actor a disservice by allowing them to continue in a process that is, by nature, unforgiving of an ill fit.

JUST remember, we're human: And as a teacher of playwriting, I have biases, prejudices, shortsightedness, sometimes impatience, and though I'm hesitant to admit it, occasional ignorance. So in any situation where I'm teaching you something you genuinely want to learn, listen to what I have to say, but don't be afraid to question me. It's good for both of us.

Well, I think that *just* about wraps it up. This has a been a theme essay. I never cared much for themes, but I think that's just my resistance to structure. Heeeeeeeeey. Now there's an idea to write about . . .

Just . . . Passing It On

By way of introduction, a short story: Big Theatre in Middle America (well, big for me—something that is bigger than a living room and has padded, bolted-in-the-floor seats) calls and says, "We read your play. We like it." I don't want to sound like Sally Field, but I do want them to continue talking. "That's great," I quickly respond.

A long pause. Did I say enough? Did I say too much? Finally she says: "So I'm passing it on." I get excited, but try to remain in that casual-sounding place of cool self-confidence: "Terrific," I say, "To whom?" She offers, "To another reader," but sounds irritated. I'm thinking she's thinking, "Isn't it enough that I said I'm passing it on?" and I'm very aware her clock is ticking. I think, "I'll pay for the call! Just keep talking." But she doesn't, and says she'll be in touch.

The waiting game. A month later comes the second call to my answering machine to tell me that the second reader *loved it*, and it's being passed on again, this time to the Literary Manager (who was the first person who called?—my mistake for not asking). Two weeks later comes another call from the Literary Manager (!) who *loved it* and is passing it on to the Artistic Director with a strong recommendation.

One week later I get my rejection letter.

One minute later I'm furious and want to kill someone.

One day later I decide to write this letter because I'm tired of people not having the sensitivity to get beyond the "Well, we've called three times with good news, but ewwwwwww, who wants to make a bad news phone call?" mentality, and I'm angry for not being treated like the professional that I'm trying hard to be. So I offer the following advice for all of us. Write your own letter, or use mine (just check it off and send it in), but let's stop emotionally colluding with people who, for whatever reason, don't understand that not having good news to give us on any level is not a reason to stop talking to us.

Dear Literary Manager/Intern/Overworked-Underpaid Best Friend to the Artistic Director Who's Reading Plays Because Somebody Has to Do It for Free:

I submitted my play to your theatre □ a week ago □ a month ago □ a year ago □ before you started working there □ well, it has been so long ago, frankly I've forgotten when it was. **And as of yet, I** □ haven't heard squat □ didn't even get the lousy postcard back I sent you □ haven't gotten my play back, a phone call, or any acknowledgment that you know who I am. **And I wonder** □ did I put enough postage on the envelope? □ did you ever read my play? □ did *anybody* ever read my play? □ did you read my play and forget to tell me? □ did you read my play six months ago, forget to write the letter, and now can't write the letter because nobody remembers what the play is about? □ did you read my play, like it, then have a reading for the public and forget to tell me? □ did you read my play, like it, pass it on to the next person who also liked it, and they passed it on, and now it's sitting in someone's house under their stack of dirty laundry?

I understand that □ money's tight □ resources are tight □ everyone's overworked □ everyone's underpaid □ you've been moving to a new location □ you've had a change of staff □ you've had a change of heart □ you've had a change of mind to read original work □ you're in production □ you're in financial ruin □ you're in the *New York Times* this week □ you got a special Tony citation last week □ you lost your funding from the NEA □ you lost your artistic director or literary manager or producer □ you lost your courage to respond because it's been so long. **And frankly** □ I don't want to appear too eager □ too needy □ too temperamental □ too difficult □ I've tried to call, but nobody seems to be able to answer my question □ I've tried writing to you, but no one responded.

BUT, please understand that I wrote something that I think is worthy of your attention. And you're a link to seeing my dream realized, so I get emotional about this kind of stuff. And though I know we're all working in tough times, when I send my work out to a theatre that □ doesn't respond in a reasonable amount of time □ doesn't respond at all □ falls out of love with me and doesn't tell me, I get angry, disappointed and bitter,

I question my career choice, and if my head's not on right, I feel defeated by an artistic system that doesn't seem to understand my value.

So what I'm asking is that you reconsider how you respond to new plays and playwrights submitting their work to you.

It's a small world, so I'm withholding my name.

PART 3

*It is not because things are difficult that we do not dare;
it is because we do not dare that they are difficult.*

Seneca

✳   ✳   ✳

FOR YO' MAMA

(This is the stuff we all want to think about so we'll know how to behave and not embarrass our poor mothers.)

✳   ✳   ✳

Behave!

To this day, I can still see Miss Rochelle (fourth-grade teacher, blood-red fingernails, six feet tall, suspiciously unmarried), tower over me with her hands on her hips, showing me all of her teeth and growling: "*Behave*, young man. You *beeeeeeee-have* or your butt is mine." I didn't flinch. I'd heard it before (kindergarten through third grade), and I'd hear it after (fifth grade through college), but somehow Miss Rochelle had a way of draining the life out of words with a voice so deep Brenda Vaccaro would sound like a soprano.

But I couldn't behave. I was too ugly to behave. I needed to stand out any way I could. That is, until I discovered the theatre in junior high school, and thought, oh, this is where all the ugly people go. There I could misbehave all I wanted and someone would applaud my effort. What a deal! I could act like the biggest idiot in the world and not only would people laugh, they'd put their hands together and make appreciative noise! I hit pre-teen pay dirt!

My newfound world came crashing down when I discovered in high school that you actually have to *behave* in the theatre too—that there was a discipline to be learned and a way of conducting oneself as an artist. I felt rooked; I wanted my money back. After all, I got into the theatre because it was the only safe place I could unleash my wild, uncontrollable energy and exorcize all of those voices, characters, and imitations I was famous for in homeroom; it was the only place I didn't have to make excuses for who I was.

Now, twenty-five years later, I see too many of my professional colleagues still embracing the idea we don't have to make excuses for how we behave. After all, we're theatre people. We don't make a lot of money. We often work under extraordinarily difficult circumstances. There's no time to be kind. There's no time or energy to be diplomatic. We've got to get the show up, finish the rewrite, get the PR out, gel the lights, put one last stitch on the hem. WHAT DO YOU MEAN, BE NICE?

It often seems that being in the theatre—being a theatre artist of any kind, or managing theatre people—allows you a certain automatic disclaimer for bad professional or personal behavior—almost as if to say, we're artists (or manage them), we're eccentric, we don't (have to) act like other people. On the artist's side, we're desperate for recognition, waiting for the big moment, our break, the reward for all of our hard work. *And*, we'll endure just about anybody's bad behavior because we don't want to appear difficult. On the manager's side (agents, artistic directors, literary managers, etc.), we're overworked, understaffed, and underpaid for our services. No one really appreciates or knows all that we do. We're a little bitter, a little angry, and very tired. The last thing we need is another buzz in our ear from a pesky fly.

So we stop being kind. We forget our humanity. We abandon our upbringing and forget our religions. To embrace this behavior as writers is a sealed death warrant for our careers. We must learn to behave well with our fellow writers, directors, literary managers, producers, and agents. *They, in turn, need to learn to behave well with us.* Granted, there are times we'd all like to hire a hit man to take someone out, but the truth is this is an industry that is built primarily on relationships; understand that and a successful career is not a given (what is?), but it is a possibility. And I don't know about you, but anything that furthers my chances is well worth investigating.

I'm on a crusade for a kinder, gentler theatre for writers. If we learn how to behave with each other—writer to writer—and we're kinder to ourselves, wouldn't it stand to follow that we could stop *attacking* our careers and actually enjoy them? It all starts with a little common sense and sensitivity.

When Someone Asks You to Read Their Play (and you do)

1. *Read the play.* Maybe I'm just being simpleminded, but *read the play.* The writer knows that play inside and out. She/he knows if you've skimmed over it or if you've actually read it. So don't say you'll read it if you can't. And don't try to bluff

your way through the discussion; the writer knows what you're doing. We are artists who base our craft in perception, so don't you think we know if you haven't read our play?

2. If life gets busy (and it always does), pick up the phone and CALL THE WRITER and say you haven't read the play. Find the courage. Do the noble thing. Yes, it's awkward. And nobody likes disappointing a friend or colleague, but nothing hurts like a promise that's ignored.

3. If you don't like kitchen realism, and the play is kitchen realism, don't read the play. Ask yourself how helpful can you be to the writer when the genre is clearly something you don't respond to. Instead, offer to find someone for the writer who in fact loves kitchen realism and is willing to read it.

4. Any writer, no matter who she/he is, comes to the experience of discussing their play a little/lot defensive. They can't help it. It's natural. They want you to like their play no matter the flaws. Your first task, then, is to take them off the defensive by saying something supportive or positive. I know it can feel artificial or insincere, but you must. It's important to the discussion that follows. Criticism is hard for all of us, and if you jump right into a discussion with the negative, the writer seldom gets beyond your first words.

5. If you're not sure how to begin the discussion, ask. Writers know what they want to talk about. Ask what would be most helpful to talk about (that's the objective, isn't it?) Ask them what they *don't need* to talk about—they're often aware of the problems you'll spend an hour talking about. Allow the writer to tell you what she/he's most concerned about dramaturgically; it takes the burden of criticism off you solely and balances it between you and the writer.

6. Observations—without some qualification—are not helpful to a writer: "I liked it," "that didn't work for me," "I don't believe the character," "the dialogue seems stiff," "the ending doesn't work," may all be accurate appraisals of the text, but it's not helpful unless you can say *why*. Be specific. If you

can't say why, don't offer it. *It's not good enough to say, "I don't know why. It's just a feeling I have."* (It's like eating Chinese food . . .)

7.   Avoid offering solutions to problems. Instead, guide the discussion to allow the writer to discover any number of solutions. If you say, "end the play this way" and they do, and at the first public reading everyone hates the ending of the play, how are you both going to feel?

8.   Make your point and get off it. Don't try to *prove* your criticism. Let the writer absorb it and move on.

9.   Don't agree to read the next draft of the play if you're really not interested. You'll find yourself in a no-win situation.

If a Friend Invites You to a Production of Their Original Play (and you go)

1.   Find the writer at the end of the evening, and say something to them. Don't sneak out. Don't convince yourself that it'll be OK to call them in the morning. Don't convince yourself that the writer doesn't really even know you're there. Trust me, they know: they've checked the reservation list a hundred times. And now that they've been publicly exposed and are incredibly vulnerable, they want some sort of reaction—even if it's just a handshake or a hug. Writers have long memories and they remember injuries.

2.   Get in touch with your humanity. No one writes a bad play on purpose. No one mounts a bad production because they want to. Chances are, if the play or production is bad, the writer knows. At the end of the evening, wouldn't it be nice to offer some kind of positive support instead of an affirmation of what the playwright already knows?

3.   Watch what you say around the theatre. You don't know who's listening to you, and who they know. People don't wear signs that say, "I'm the playwright's mother," or "I'm her agent." Secondhand criticism (information given to a playwright that's overheard) is like a bullet in the dark: you never

see it coming so it's twice as destructive because it's from a stranger that you have no connection to.

4. Unless writers solicit your criticism at the end of the evening, don't give it. They won't/can't hear it then. They're high from the success, or depressed because of the problems. Just make a date to talk.

5. If you're a friend, and you leave at intermission, your legs should be broken.

I know so much of this sounds like common sense—but there's the rub. Our common sense leaves us under pressure, strain, eagerness, or exuberance, or is frankly something that we never associate with our art. I have to think that we're all capable of doing what we do and still maintaining our humanity and caring for one another—of behaving. I guess I could blame it on Miss Rochelle, and on all those teachers before and after her who uttered that word to me that would resonate in my soul (creative, or otherwise) for the rest of my life. But I'd rather think that I learned somewhere, in some small corner of my experiences, that being a gentleperson and being treated kindly by a gentleperson could only enhance the quality of my life . . . and certainly my art.

Slap Yourself

I've been writing a long time. And I've been teaching as long as I've been writing. So I've heard it all. Nothing surprises me. And if I haven't heard it, God knows I've said it myself. So the next time you're tempted to utter these words, or even think about saying them, do us all a favor: just slap yourself. Yup, rear back and pop yourself one. Alright, so you'll rob me of the fantasy of doing it myself to you, but it'll be safe that way. (Sometimes I'm too impulsive for my own good.)

Well, I meant for the first scene to be confusing. Wait a minute, wait a minute. You meant to confuse me? You wanted me to not know what the hell was going on in the first twenty minutes of your play because I'd be so satisfied when I'm illuminated in the last hour?! Forget about it! I've already checked out. I'm thinking about whether I should have tacos or enchiladas for dinner. And I'm pissed at you for wasting my time. I don't want to be confused! Challenged, yes. Stimulated, yes. Surprised, yes. Confused, no.

I know the first act's way too long, but the second act's short. I don't care! Too long is too long. Cut the damn thing before you show it to anyone. Have a private reading and decide what needs to go. Don't subject me to what you know is an obvious problem. I'm not that forgiving or generous with my time.

I know I didn't actually have a production at the Guthrie, but it was a reading in the hallway with some actors, so I was at the Guthrie. Bottom line: a reading is *not* a production. A production is a production. Don't lie. Don't say you've been produced somewhere you haven't. This is a small world we work in, and everybody knows everybody. Eventually, your lie will surface and you'll look ignorant, deceitful, or both.

The reading of my play was horrible because the director didn't really get the play, the actors weren't connected, the lighting was bad on stage, and the woman sitting next to me was breathing so loud I couldn't hear a line of my dialogue. This could all be true, but where are you in the equation? There is a way to reflect back on a disappointing experience without decimating everyone involved with it.

Susan ruined the first act. She didn't wait for the laugh on her exit line, mumbled the next line, and the whole audience didn't understand what was going on. If what I need to understand the action of your play rests on one moment or one line, we're in trouble.

They (the audience) just didn't get it. You mean, the whole audience didn't get it? All those people and not one person understood what you wrote? Wow. That's remarkable. Wonder why?

I know it doesn't really make sense, but I like the way the words sound together in that line. Are you trying to confuse me again? Why do you want to confuse me? I don't want to be confused!

He read it like, blah blah blah. If the actor will read it like, BLAH BLAH BLAH, it'll make sense. Maybe, maybe not. It's for the director and actor to discover. You make sure the writing's clear.

I don't have a point of view in the play. I want the audience to fill it in. That's about the silliest thing I've ever heard.

It's not very good, but could you read it anyway?. Sure, I've got all the time in the world. Not to worry. I'd love to muddle through what you already think is bad.

Oh, his play wasn't so great. I could write that. OK. Go ahead. Do it. That's about as insensitive and shortsighted as me standing in the Metropolitan Museum of Art, looking up at any of the abstract painters of our century and saying, "Oh, I could do that. It's just a lot of paint on a canvas."

I know it has problems, but I want to hear it just as I wrote it. No, I'm sorry. I don't want to witness you doing your homework. Do your homework, then call me in to hear your play read.

I don't know how I do it. I just sit down and out it comes. No comment.

An Open Letter to Those Who Love and Support Us

Xerox it or cut it out. Send it. Sometimes, they just don't get it . . .

Dear □ Mom, Dad, Brother, Sister, or any combination therein, □ sweetheart, □ best friend, □ new friend, □ would-be friend, □ Teacher, □ Mentor:

I know it's difficult sometimes for you to understand what I'm doing by being a playwright. I know you think □ there's no money in it □ no future in it □ no husband or wife to be found in it □ no sense in it □ it's frivolous □ a lofty dream □ I'm on drugs and in an altered state of reality □ I watched too much television, **and that in your best estimation, I** □ am wasting my time □ wasting your money □ wasting Grandma's inheritance □ being a foolish dreamer □ don't have what it takes to be a writer □ should be pursuing a law degree—like my brother, sister, father, mother, uncle, aunt, next-door neighbor, the mailman before the accident. **But you have to realize that I've been given a gift to see the world differently than you do, and I want to share my own special kind of wisdom with an appreciative audience that I hope you can be a part of.**

It's □ hard □ lonely □ frustrating □ frightening □ _____ **to be at this place in my development as a playwright, and frankly, I need** □ all the love I can get □ support □ encouragement □ food □ money to pay my electric bill □ a phone call □ a letter □ your attendance at my reading or production □ all the understanding I can get. **What I don't need right now are your** □ doubts □ worries □ values □ beliefs □ judgments □ criticisms □ disrespect □ reminders that I'll never make it □ reminders that I failed the last time I tried something like this □ reminders that I'm not like another writer you know □ reminders that I'm not like anyone else in my family or any person within a fifty-mile radius of our home.

For someone who uses language as a tool of my trade, sometimes words fail me and I don't know how to say what I need to say to you. But I'm depending on you to see me through, to believe in me, and to offer me your

love and encouragement at a time I need it the most. I can't make any promises that I'll be everything you want me to be, or even what I want me to be. But I do know that I'm trying hard, with all my heart and soul, to do well. Isn't that all you can ask of anybody?

So the next time you □ call □ write □ run into me at school □ run into me in the aisle at the grocery store □ see me at Joseph's bar mitzvah □ invite me to dinner □ invite me to church □ invite me home for the holidays even though it was a disaster the last nine times I was at home, **do me one simple favor: ask me, "How's your writing going?"** I may be awkward the first couple of times you ask—I'm not used to talking about it with those I love and care for—but be patient. I'll answer your question. And if I don't, don't remind me of this letter. Just understand that I need you to help me feel comfortable in my own doubts.

Thanks for listening. It feels good to know I've shared my feelings with someone I care about so much.

LOVE, _____

P.S.: I just □ started a new play □ finished a rewrite of an old play □ heard the first draft of my play in class □ finally understood what I'm trying to write about in my new play □ had a director approach me about directing my play □ heard that Theatre in the Oak Trees is doing my one-act. **I'm real happy. Wish me luck.**

After Words

Playwrights are special. We're different and we're special. We see the poetry of the sun hanging in the sky, the comedy in a funeral, and the drama in ants scurrying toward their hole in the ground before the rain. We study and stare at things most people simply pass by. We comb through our feelings like a thick head of hair, pulling at the tangles until they're freed. We create great, elaborate fantasies, full of intense psychodrama and muted psychotherapy. We push our feelings away from us, hoping someone will recognize the honesty in what we feel and pet our wounded psyches. We laugh at the same memory that often makes us cry, and weep at the anger in another. We understand the complexity of a given emotion, a given moment in time, and an uncertain circumstance. We imitate what we see and hold it back up for the world to see and celebrate its own wisdom or to learn not to make the same mistakes over and over again. We hide behind our many disguises, shocked when someone sees us through our own veils of disbelief and disappointment. We write because we have to. We write for the theatre because the heart of man needs us to.

We are the starting point for all good and great theatre. Nothing begins without us—the craftspeople of the written word. As we fulfill our own fantasies, we help realize the fantasies of other artists: the aspiring actor, the tenacious scene designer, the determined director, or the hopeful costumer. We bring other like-minded artists together, build families from our dreams, and invite the rest of the world to see through all of our eyes the wonder and grandeur that is so uniquely us, so uniquely them. We better the world with our insights. So write well, my friends.